# Simon Ste[phens]

## Plays

### One Minute, Country Music
### Motortown, Pornography, Sea Wall

*One Minute*: 'Set in London in the aftermath of the disappearance of an eleven-year-old girl, *One Minute* brings together the girl's mother, an unreliable witness, a student/barmaid and two investigating officers . . . the writing cleverly suggests how much the characters would like to connect but never really can.' *Guardian*

*Country Music* 'spotlights four fateful moments in the life of Jamie Carris, an engaging but violent south Londoner. The play unfolds in a series of tightly focused two-handers, set before, during and after the prison sentences he has served for glassing one man and for killing another.' *Independent*

*Motortown*: 'Danny – a squaddie who has served in Basra – is bringing the war back home [to] an England where the "war on terror" has become a war waged using the tactics of the terrorists. It is also a place of dubious moralities, small-time arms dealers and middle-class swingers and anti-war protesters. A searingly honest play written with a deadly coiled energy.' *Guardian*

*Pornography*: 'Set in July 2005, between the announcement that London had been awarded the Olympics and the July 7 bombings, it tells seven entwining stories, including the imagined story of one of the bombers journeying towards London to commit an act of terrorism.' *Guardian*

*Sea Wall*: 'A quietly gripping monologue about grief and belief . . . this play is like a deceptive calm blue sea beneath which lurks a ferocious riptide of sorrow.' *Guardian*

**Simon Stephens** is a British writer whose theatrical career began in the literary department of the Royal Court Theatre where he ran its Young Writers' Programme. His plays for theatre include *Bluebird* (Royal Court Theatre, 1998); *Herons* (Royal Court, 2001); *Port* (Royal Exchange Theatre, Manchester 2002); *One Minute* (Crucible Theatre, Sheffield, 2003, Bush Theatre, 2004); *Christmas* (Bush Theatre, 2004); *Country Music* (Royal Court, 2004); *On the Shore of the Wide World* (Royal Exchange, Manchester, and National Theatre, 2005); *Motortown* (Royal Court, 2006); *Pornography* (Deutsches Schauspielhaus, Hanover, 2007, and Birmingham Repertory Theatre, 2008). His radio plays include *Five Letters Home to Elizabeth* (BBC Radio 4, 2001) and *Digging* (BBC Radio 4, 2003). Awards include the Pearson Award for Best Play, 2001, for *Port*; Olivier Award for Best New Play for *On the Shore of the Wide World*, 2005, and for *Motortown* German Critics in Theater Heute's annual poll voted him Best Foreign Playwright, 2007. His screenwriting includes *Jackdaw* and he is currently developing an original series for Channel 4.

*by the same author*

Christmas
Harper Regan
Herons
On the Shore of the Wide World
Port

STEPHENS PLAYS: I
(Bluebird, Christmas, Herons, Port)

SIMON STEPHENS

# Plays: 2

**One Minute
Country Music
Motortown
Pornography
Sea Wall**

*with an introduction by the author*

Bloomsbury Methuen Drama
An imprint of Bloomsbury Publishing Plc

B L O O M S B U R Y
LONDON · NEW DELHI · NEW YORK · SYDNEY

**Bloomsbury Methuen Drama**

An imprint of Bloomsbury Publishing Plc

Imprint previously known as Methuen Drama

| | |
|---|---|
| 50 Bedford Square | 1385 Broadway |
| London | New York |
| WC1B 3DP | NY 10018 |
| UK | USA |

www.bloomsbury.com

This collection first published in Great Britain in 2009 by Methuen Drama
Reprinted 2010 (twice), 2012, 2013, 2014

One Minute first published by Methuen Drama in 2003
Revised in this volume. © 2003, 2009 Simon Stephens
Country Music first published by Methuen Publishing Limited in 2004
Revised in this volume. © 2004, 2009 Simon Stephens
Motortown first published by Methuen Drama in 2006
Revised in this volume. © 2006, 2009 Simon Stephens
Pornography first published by Methuen Drama in 2008
Revised in this volume. © 2008, 2009 Simon Stephens
Sea Wall first published by Methuen Drama in 2009
© 2009 Simon Stephens

Introduction © 2009 Simon Stephens

**British Library Cataloguing-in-Publication Data**
A catalogue record for this book is available from the British Library.

| ISBN: PB: | 978-1-4081-1391-2 |
|---|---|
| ePDF: | 978-1-4081-4582-1 |
| ePub: | 978-1-4081-1478-0 |

**Library of Congress Cataloging-in-Publication Data**
A catalog record for this book is available from the Library of Congress.

Series: Contemporary Dramatists

Printed and bound in Great Britain

# Contents

Contents

# Simon Stephens
# Chronology

| | |
|---|---|
| 1997 | *Bring Me Sunshine* (Assembly Rooms, Edinburgh, and Riverside Studio, London) |
| 1998 | *Bluebird* (Royal Court, London) |
| 2001 | *Herons* (Royal Court): nominated for the Olivier Award for Most Promising Playwright |
| | *Five Letters to Elizabeth* (radio play, broadcast on BBC Radio 4) |
| 2002 | *Port* (Royal Exchange, Manchester): Pearson Award for Best New Play in 2001/2 |
| 2003 | *Digging* (radio play, broadcast on BBC Radio 4) |
| | *One Minute* (produced by the Actors Touring Company, Crucible Theatre, Sheffield) |
| 2003/4 | *Christmas* (Pavilion Theatre, Brighton, and Bush Theatre, London) |
| 2004 | *Country Music* (Royal Court) |
| 2005 | *On the Shore of the Wide World* (Royal Exchange Manchester, and National Theatre, London): Olivier Award for Best New Play in 2005 |
| 2006 | *Motortown* (Royal Court) |
| 2007 | *Pornography* (Deutsches Schauspielhaus, Hanover) |
| 2008 | *Harper Regan* (National Theatre) |
| | *Pornography* (Edinburgh Traverse Theatre, and Birmingham Repertory Theatre) |
| | *Sea Wall* (Bush Theatre) |

# Introduction

In the autumn of 2001 I worked at Wandsworth prison, in
south London, teaching a course in playwriting. It was set
up with the director Esther Baker whose theatre company
Synergy specialises in working with prisoners. I taught with
their creative-writing teacher, the playwright and political
activist Anders Lustgarten.

Before I started I was terrified at the prospect. I'd had,
since childhood, a recurring dream of being sent to prison.
I have no doubt this is quite a common dream. I can't
identify its specific starting point for me, though. Maybe it
was the clang of the gates on the opening credits of *Porridge*
that I watched as a kid. Probably it was something slightly
darker than that. But whatever started it, there was something
about prisons, especially those huge urban Victorian prisons
dotted around London, that chilled me. The finality of the
close of those doors and the size of those locks was horrifying.
It was a horror that ran through me when I first arrived at
Wandsworth.

My terrified nervousness wasn't relaxed by the guards on
the desk there, who were officious at best, unfriendly often
and occasionally downright aggressive. Nor by the fact that
our sessions were to be carried out, Esther informed me, in
the basement near where the gallows used to be. It was a
nervousness that was, in fact, only eased by the charm and
cheeriness of the prisoners.

I worked with a group of about twelve men in total.
Mostly they were in there on short or medium sentences.
Mostly the sentences were for crimes of drug dealing or
fraud. The men were sensitive to my nerves and seemed
grateful to me for my commitment to teaching them. None
more so than Ali, an avuncular Asian Londoner in his early
thirties. He was a sharp writer, a good reader and a real wit.

I remember Ali most for one session in particular.

One morning, about halfway through the course, the
guys were unusually late coming down from the wing. They
were often five or ten minutes late but on this day I'd been

waiting for about twenty minutes before the first of them
arrived. It was Ali. He bounded in to the room. Shook my
hand. There was a particular energy about him. 'Did you
hear what happened?' he asked me. I'd been travelling for
the last hour. I'd heard nothing. 'This plane flew into the
World Trade Center.' It sounded like the opening line of a
joke. Knowing Ali as I did, I expected it to be a very good
joke so I awaited its punchline. A few moments later the
head of education came to tell us that another plane had
flown into the second tower. Ali's face broke into an
astonished grin. 'It's my brethren,' he said, smiling ironically
as he went to sit down to get ready to start the session.

Four years later I was writing *Motortown*, the third play in
this collection, at home in east London. It was a warm
morning. The writing was going fairly well. I'd had a good
day's work the previous day, punctuated, or energised
rather, by the news that London's bid to host the Olympic
Games in 2012 had been successful. The kids were at
school. My wife was at the gym. I had the house to myself.
I'd drunk about three cups of coffee so I stopped work to
have a piss. I put the radio on. The morning phone-in on
5 Live had been interrupted by discussion of a power surge
all over the London Underground. Then a young man rang
the station to report that a friend calling him from Russell
Square, in the centre of London, had just woken him up. A
bus had exploded. It wasn't a power surge that was affecting
the Underground, the caller suggested, it was a terrorist
attack. The phone-in host made it clear that the caller's
claims were entirely speculative. Two minutes later Reuters
confirmed his speculation as fact.

The five plays in this collection have been informed by
many experiences. They've been informed by the birth of my
second son and first daughter, Stanley and Scarlet. They've
been informed by watching them and my eldest son Oscar
grow. They've been informed by my eventual marriage to
my long-term girlfriend, the beautiful, long-suffering,
brilliant Polly. They've been informed by teaching on the
Young Writers Programme at the Royal Court between
2001 and 2006, and by the many actors and directors I've

worked with and writers I've talked to, hung out with, taught with and whose work I've read and watched. But, more than the four plays that came before them, these plays were informed by those two ruptures.

Gordon Anderson directed my play *Bluebird* when it was staged in the 1998 Young Writers Festival at the Royal Court. In 2001 he was made artistic director of the Actors Touring Company, and commissioned me to write a play for him. More than any commission I've had, my work on *One Minute* was collaborative. Gordon and I spent quite a bit of time in various pubs around London deciding what type of play we wanted to make. We wanted to write about the city. We wanted, too, to write about grief. He encouraged me to be formally bolder than I'd previously been. He told me to write a play that worked with the same spirit of juxta-position as an album does. Many writers working in Europe at the turn of the millennium inspired him, especially the German-language playwrights Rainald Goetz and Franz Xavier Kroetz, and he gave me play after play to read. He also wanted to develop the play through workshops.

Over a period of about six weeks spread over perhaps eight months, initially at the Actors Centre and then at the ATC offices, and using improvisations and interviews, writing and acting exercises we worked with actors to imagine situations, settings, characters and objectives. On the back of these workshops I would go home and write.

The play I wrote became a curious kind of detective story. Touched by the abduction and murder of schoolgirl Milly Dowling in 2002, the play told the story of the police search for a missing child. If *One Minute* was a detective story, though, it was a detective story with its centre removed, with its heart taken out. Many of the scenes that one imagines when considering a dramatised police missing persons search were taken away. There was never a body revealed onstage. No suspect was identified. No one was arrested or interrogated. There was no confession. No one was ever charged or sentenced. The case remained open. Partly this was a response to the demands of theatre, and partly, to a

degree, a response to the limitations of a touring production.
But it was more than those things, I think.

The play is more of a meditation on grief than it is a cop
story. Whenever I have grieved, and whenever I have
watched people grieving, I am always struck by the notion
that the core has been removed from their lives. It's like
they've had a part of them taken away. This is an image
I would return to later in *Sea Wall*. I wanted to find a form,
in *One Minute*, that dramatised the absence as much as the
drama of the detective story.

Over the past six years this search for a form has been
central to my work. The question of how dramatists articulate
or release ideas informs much contemporary critical debate
around new writing. There is a generation of critics and
writers and directors who retain a loyalty to the form of play
that addresses idea through utterance or statement. Such
statement is normally delivered in lengthy, often beautiful,
speeches about four-fifths of the way through a play. Normally
by the play's central protagonist. I find this limiting. In the
plays in this collection I've tried as much as possible to use
dramatic structure or form, linguistic register or visual
images, or more often the contradictory juxtaposition of
these elements, to dramatise that which I want to say. I find
that such juxtaposition creates plays that demand a position
of interpretation from their audience rather than reception.
As an audience member I always enjoy creatively
investigating an idea rather than simply listening to one.

I worked with Gordon again in 2004 when Ian Rickson,
the then artistic director of the Royal Court, asked him to
direct my commissioned play *Country Music*. This was the play
I wrote in response to my experiences teaching playwriting
to prisoners. It was Ian who'd suggested to me the idea of
working with prisoners. Since 1979 the theatre company
Clean Break has established a tradition of playwrights
working with female prisoners. Many fine plays continue to
come from this company and this work. But women make
up maybe 10 per cent of the prison population of the UK.
No similar work had been carried out for male prisoners.

After my eight weeks at Wandsworth culminated in a rehearsed reading of the prisoners' work, I repeated the workshops at HMP Grendon in Buckinghamshire. This was and remains a remarkable institution. It's the only therapeutic prison in the country for male offenders. Every week the inmates at Grendon carry out approximately twenty hours of group therapy. It is a far less foreboding institution than Wandsworth, both in terms of its architecture and its hierarchy. Here, inmates call the wardens by their first names and wardens remain friendly, chatty and on good terms with the inmates as much as they do with the guests and teachers at the prison. It's also a very successful institution with a within-ten-year reoffending rate of 30 per cent against a national average of 70 per cent. But the tone of the workshops in each prison was striking. My abiding memory of working at Wandsworth was the amount of fun I had. We seemed to spend much of our time there, the writers and me, laughing. Whereas at Wandsworth the writers were mainly serving short-term sentences, at Grendon the sentences were usually far longer and the crimes were predominantly of a violent or sexual nature. The tone of the workshops was less ribald. It was sadder.

Like Wandsworth, the work at Grendon culminated with a rehearsed reading. If the culmination was a blast at Wandsworth, at Grendon it was an extraordinary day. Under the direction of Dawn Walton, eight actors from the Royal Court came and performed the scenes that the men had written to the entire population of the prison. It was an audience of around a hundred men, many of whom, I later learned, had come with the intention of mocking or even spoiling the presentation. They made a threatening bunch. Over the three months of the course I'd become so comfortable with the writers in my group that it was often easy to forget that they were serving time for violent criminal activity. It was easy to remember that when looking at their audience. They looked frankly murderous.

And yet the calibre of the writing and the commitment of the performances were so strong that every member of the audience watching it was moved. Their laughter was genuine.

One writer told me that making the audience laugh with his
play was unlike any other experience he'd had. For a short
time, he told me, it felt like he was free. And when the same
audience watched a heartbreaking, largely autobiographical
piece about a child visiting his father at Grendon on the day
the prison put aside for family visits, I was taken aback to
see this audience of huge, brooding, violent men so palpably
touched.

*Country Music* spans twenty years in the life of a man called
Jamie Carris. It is a play about chances not taken. Every
man I worked with at Wandsworth and Grendon, and every
boy I worked with on the young offenders' teams while
teaching on the Young Writers' Programme, touched me
with their potential and by that potential's frustration. I
would leave those places desperately sad. The men I worked
with were capable of extraordinary acts of imagination as
much as they were capable of crimes. At various points
in their lives they'd made mistakes. The irreversibility of
those mistakes was haunting. Especially at Grendon it was
clear that men whose behaviour was often surprising,
contradictory, alive, alert, were defined by singular
moments where their behaviour had been brutal. Defined
by one moment they were unable ever to redefine themselves
as anything else. There was something awful about this I
wanted to dramatise.

I listen to music constantly. I'm inspired to write by it.
Often my intention at the start of conceiving a play will be
to have the same impact on an audience member as a piece
of music has on me. I've loved country music since hearing
Elvis Costello's *Almost Blue* album as a teenager. The play
and the musical form have much in common. They deal
with similar themes of regret, self-abuse, violence and flight.
They share simplicity of form. I've often been staggered by
the emotional range that country music singers can achieve
in three chords and one and a half minutes, and wanted to
aspire to such simplicity and brevity and to the tension
between that simplicity and brevity and that emotional
range with my play. Also, many country songs, taking their
lead from hymns, finish with a refrain of the opening verse.

So the play returns to the beginning and to Jamie Carris's first flawed decision and wasted opportunity.

It is a short play that spans a considerable time, and demands, from the actor playing Jamie, a performance of real nuance and range. I was lucky that Gordon Anderson, as he had done with *One Minute*, directed *Country Music* with such precision and that at the heart of the play was a stunning performance from Lee Ross.

In its final week we took the production into the same gallows area of Wandsworth prison where I'd taught two years earlier. An administrative error meant that by the time we arrived in the jail the audience of sixty prisoners had been waiting for ten minutes, exasperated by the fact that their important education sessions were to be replaced by the performance of a play that none of them had heard of, had any interest in watching, and that didn't appear to be happening at all. For all of us, especially Sally Hawkins and Laura Elphinstone, two young actresses in the company, it was a daunting audience to walk right into.

The performance the company gave that afternoon, to an audience that had initially been hostile and which were typically unforgiving of tedium or pretentiousness, was shattering. The silence in the scene between Lee and Callum Callaghan as Jamie's brother Matty, or later the confrontation he had with his daughter, played by Laura, was electrifying. I'd never seen an audience more alert to something they'd resisted, probably an alertness born out of self-recognition. This self-recognition, it seems to me, is one of the things that theatre can offer its audience. There is something rather dignified about it, I think.

Ian Rickson also played an instrumental part in the writing of *Motortown*. We talked about the way in which music had inspired *Country Music* and the following play *On the Shore of the Wide World*. Ian told me that every play I'd written to date had evoked the same spirit in him as was evoked by ballads. He wanted me to write a play that had the same acerbic dissonant energy as those bands I'd loved since adolescence, like the Fall and the Butthole Surfers.

I enjoy writing commissions. I find the kind of intervention that Ian made with both *Country Music* and *Motortown* inspirational. I also enjoy writing for specific stages and specific theatres. *Motortown* was the fourth play of mine that the Royal Court produced. The tradition of dissidence, abrasion and challenge at that theatre and its equally lengthy tradition of self-criticism have always spurred me on. I wanted to write something that engaged with that tradition.

My office at the Young Writers' Programme was temporarily moved to a dressing room adjoining the Theatre Downstairs at the Court at the time of writing. Like many of my favourite theatres, the Theatre Downstairs manages to be both epic and intimate at the same time. The grandeur of its proscenium disguises the fact that it is possible to whisper on the stage and yet be clearly heard. The proscenium is a theatrical architecture that in itself touches plays with tradition. That specific Court stage has more tradition than most. Watching any play there it is impossible to forget Beckett or Osborne or Bond or Churchill or Kane. As I worked, I couldn't help thinking that it was a stage that was at its finest when empty. I would sometimes feel bereft when expensive sets were built that stopped me from seeing that beautiful back wall. *Motortown* was written to be performed on that stage and is performed best, I think, when the set is as spare as possible.

I love spare stages. I love seeing the infrastructure and the mess and business of theatres revealed to me. I love watching actors become characters. I love then watching them become actors again. I love it because it demands from me as an audience member an engagement with the fact that what I am watching is fundamentally metaphorical. It's made up.

If I've often written for stages and theatres I've also often written for actors. When I imagine a scene in my head I don't see fictional characters in a real world. I see actors, often actors I know, playing on real stages. I saw the Theatre Downstairs at the Royal Court in writing *Motortown*. I also saw Danny Mays. He's an actor I've known for a few years. He combines a sparkling intuitive intelligence with a physical suppleness and an emotional vulnerability that is startling. The role of Danny, the play's protagonist, a psychologically damaged Iraq War veteran returning home to Dagenham, was written for him. Subsequent productions of the play have revealed to me how essential it is that the actor playing Danny must be immediately likeable. We need to fall in love with him. If we can recognise ourselves in him in the opening three scenes we're forced to recognise ourselves in him as the play progresses and his behaviour becomes more troubling.

I wanted *Motortown* to be a play that troubled its audience. It was important to me that a play that looked at such a brutal, ghastly war should take a position that maybe undermined the expectations of the Court's largely liberal regulars. There was something about the anti-war movement that built up around the declaration of war in Iraq that unnerved me. It was a movement that seemed to be based on a separation of the war from the international context that surrounded it. It managed, at times, to argue its way into defending the sovereignty of a mass murderer. I was not an unapologetic advocate of the war in any way and was sensitive to many arguments made against it. But it struck me as simplistic and somehow childlike not to see the war as symptomatic rather than causal. It wasn't that the war was a monstrosity born out of a salvageable world. The world felt malign to me. The war seemed symptomatic of that. And it gave me no end of pleasure that the play was at various times, by various critics, received as being a criticism of the war and a criticism of the anti-war campaign.

*Motortown*, conceived over six months but written over four days, is the play I was writing on 7 July 2005 when four bombs exploded on the London transport system. It was a period of time I returned to that autumn for *Pornography*, the fourth play in this collection.

I've been lucky enough to have several productions of my plays outside England. These productions have predominantly taken place in German-speaking countries. The first of those was a production of *Herons*, directed in Basel and Stuttgart by Swiss director Sebastian Nübling. When Stuttgart's

artistic director Friedrich Schirmer took over the Deutsches
Schauspielhaus in Hamburg, he invited Sebastian to work
there with him. He asked Sebastian what he wanted to
direct. Sebastian was keen for the theatre to commission a
new play from me.

The Deutsches Schauspielhaus is a huge theatre with over
a thousand seats, its neo-baroque style the work of Viennese
architects Fellner and Hellmer who together designed several
of the major theatres in the German-speaking world. It was
a daunting stage to write for. If I had any instinct it was that
this was a theatre that suited individual performances more
than it suited crowd scenes. On epic stages epic stories are
made more grand by being refracted through individual
voices.

One of my abiding memories of living in London at the
time of the terrorist attacks and the second wave of failed
attacks that followed a fortnight later was an inability to
share many people's incredulity. I couldn't share others'
horror that the boys who bombed London were British by
birth. Rather, it seemed logical to me. Their actions seemed
to be absolutely a product of the same Britain I'd grown up
in. They were born and raised in a Britain built by one prime
minister who denied altogether the existence of society and
another who made a passionate plea for understanding to
be valued less than unthinking condemnation of others. I
wanted to write a play that put a terrorist action on equal
footing with many of the other flaws and ruptures I saw
around me. The play is built around seven parts, each part
inspired by one of the seven ages of man, that stoical
medieval philosophy so forcefully articulated by Jaques in
*As You Like It*. Each of the seven parts dramatises a story of
transgression. The transgression of suicidal mass murder sits
in the same spectrum, albeit on a far more extreme position
on that spectrum, as do the others in the play.

If *Motortown* was written with an actor as well as a theatre
in mind, then *Pornography* was written with a director in
mind. I had watched many of Sebastian's productions on
video, and come to know him around the time he did

*Herons*. Drunkenly in a bar in Hamburg one time, I told him I was going to write him a play that would be both a present and a gauntlet. I wanted to write something that awoke his lively sense of play. He has a remarkable visual eye. He works brilliantly with direct audience address. He also has an instinct for exploding and reworking texts in ways that no director I know in Britain would dare. I wanted to write something that would allow him to do that. So I wrote him a text that was as open as possible. It not only invites directorial interpretation, it is unstageable without it. There are only a few stage directions and they are frankly impenetrable. There are no character names. It is a play that can be staged in any order using any number of actors.

These were decisions that seemed to bewilder many readers in England. It was three years after the original production that *Pornography* was staged in the UK, and as I write this introduction it has yet to be staged in London at all. They were decisions I wouldn't have been able to make if I hadn't come to know and to work with, to befriend and collaborate with theatre practitioners across the German-speaking countries. Theirs is a theatre culture that has no fear of art or formal boldness. It is a theatre culture that values the metaphorical and the visual. I've often heard British theatre practitioners describe British theatre as the best in the world. The same people making those claims often mock the experimental nature of German theatre. I can't share their confidence in their own industries or their contempt for others. I've loved the theatre I've watched in Germany. It has nourished me. It sits most directly under *Pornography* but has informed every play I've written since.

The Bush Theatre in London's Shepherd's Bush is one of my favourite small theatres. Nested above an increasingly inhospitable pub, it has launched the careers of many of British theatre's key writers, directors and actors. It is soaked in as much history as it feels soaked in shit lager. I love it.

In 2008 it was in need of serious architectural repair, a need made more urgent by a summer of torrential rain.

In order to carry out that repair it would be necessary to remove the theatre's seating and lighting rig. Rather than closing the theatre down, though, Josie Rourke, the artistic director, asked a group of writers to submit pieces that could be performed in natural light. I wanted to write a monologue for her. I wanted to write about a sudden death. I wanted to write about fathering a daughter. I wanted to write about my increasing atheism.

I developed much of my idea for the monologue while on holiday with my wife and kids and father-in-law in France. On returning from this holiday I received an email from a friend of mine, the Irish actor Andrew Scott. I received it the morning I sat down to write. I decided to write the piece for him. I imagined his voice speaking the words. I imagined him telling my story.

Often it takes years for a play to move from commission to production. *Sea Wall* was commissioned by email on 7 August 2008. It opened, directed with nuance and subtlety, in a ripped-out, dark Bush Theatre, on 6 October and closed on 14 October. Andrew Scott was exactly as compelling as I'd hoped he would be.

Ramin Gray told me once that one of his favourite elements of theatre was that in its very form it incorporated a notion of death. Never was this death and the life that charged up to it more striking than in the conception and production of *Sea Wall*. It felt appropriate for a play that looked at the startling brutality of sudden death.

> 'You make beauty and it disappears. I love that.'
> Caryl Churchill, *Far Away*

As I write this introduction the world is reeling again from an act of terrorism. Over the past few days a series of attacks across the Indian financial capital of Mumbai have killed nearly two hundred people. I grew up with a childhood terror of what form the Third World War would take. On days like this it feels like the Third World War started without anybody telling anybody else.

Rereading these plays, it strikes me, born as they are out of this decade in which this war has raged so expensively and with such an increasing death toll and with no apparent end in sight, that they refract their time in ways that surprise me.

They are plays touched by a need for contact. The characters seem to be constantly trying to touch someone. Or reeling from that touch. Sometimes they disguise this need for contact externally by making other people drinks and food. There is a huge amount of consumption going on in these plays, whether it's the tea of *One Minute*, or the sweets of *Country Music*, the smoothies of *Motortown*, or the cigarettes of *Pornography*, and nearly all of this consumption is a metaphor for a need to touch others or receive touch. Sometimes, scorched by that touch, or agonised by its absence, characters resort to violence.

The plays often sit this need for communication or a need for emotion against institutions, the prisons of *Country Music*, the army of *Motortown* and *Sea Wall*, or the professional protocols of workplaces in *One Minute* or *Pornography*, where such emotion and such need is inappropriate and contained.

Many of the characters in these plays seem horrified or startled by their own bodies. Often, at times of trauma or enlightenment, their senses raised, they seem to notice themselves for the first time. Often they are repelled by what they realise. Feet bleed onto socks. People want to cut off their own hair or are disgusted by their own smells. The mouth seems to be peculiarly horrifying in both *Country Music* and *Motortown*. In these plays a fear of dentists is matched by a memory of wasps on the tongue.

In all of the plays I've been drawn to the duologue as a means of distilling worlds. In three of them this has been distilled further into the monologue. There are many reasons for this, but among them must be an interest in dramatising a world that seems to be more atomised and fractured than it has been in the past and subsequently scorched by a need and an inability to connect.

London dominates the landscape of these plays, even those that play out their action away from its centre. London is my home. It's where I've lived now for fifteen years. My children were all born in its East End. I can think of nowhere else I'd rather live. I miss it when I leave it. I love coming home. But I can think of nowhere else where that atomisation and that fracturing is more palpable.

All five of these plays revolve in different ways around the violent death of children. This speaks much about my anxieties as a parent but also much about the times in which the plays were written. Every time I turn on the news or read a paper now I have the unsettling sense that something seems to have gone wrong here. Something is awry. Nowhere is this clearer than in the way we seem to be treating our children. I wanted, I think, in writing these plays, to look as hard as I could into the darkness of this treatment and allow it to speak metaphorically for the world in which such treatment is played out.

Likewise, all five plays seem to have prominent moments of lengthy silence. I love silence and stillness onstage. I love the way it concentrates our gaze on the characters whose stories they tell. Theatre is the most human of all art forms. It is collaborative in its production and its reception. Its subject is innately what it is to be a human being. It is important to say that I retain as much faith in the possibilities of what human beings can achieve as I despair at what they seem to be capable of. If there is light in a theatre then it is reflected most compellingly off the people onstage, and in that there is, more often than I'd realised in these plays, possibility and hope.

Simon Stephens
December 2008

# One Minute

For Ben, Sara and Archie.
And dedicated also to Laura.

*One Minute* was first performed at the Crucible Theatre, Sheffield, on 6 June 2003. The cast was as follows:

| | |
|---|---|
| **Marie Louise Burdett** | Lucy Black |
| **Catherine Denham** | Sarah Paul |
| **Dr Anne Schults** | Teresa Banham |
| **DI Gary Burroughs** | Simon Wolfe |
| **DC Robert Evans** | Tom Ellis |

| | |
|---|---|
| *Director* | Gordon Anderson |
| *Designer* | Anthony Macilwaine |
| *Composer* | Julian Swales |
| *Lighting* | Nigel Edwards |

## Characters

**Marie Louise Burdett**, *twenty-seven*
**Catherine Denham**, *twenty-one*
**Dr Anne Schults**, *thirty-six*
**DI Gary Burroughs**, *thirty-eight*
**DC Robert Evans**, *twenty-four*

## Setting

The play is set in a variety of locations in London, over the course of 2001.

The set should be as spare as possible.

A character who plays in two consecutive scenes need not wait to arrive in any second setting before playing the second scene. Rather the scenes can bleed, quite quickly, into one another.

The characters should remain onstage throughout.

The dates could be displayed or announced before each section starts.

During the blackouts the silhouettes of the characters should become gradually clear.

The silences could be punctuated. Perhaps brief, intrusive, warning beeps. The kind of sound that fax machines make when they run out of paper.

A dash ( – ) after a word denotes an interruption or an inability to speak or complete a word or sentence. An ellipsis (. . .) denotes a trailing-off.

## January

*Blackout. Ten seconds.*

*A clothes shop on High Street Kensington. Midday.* **Marie Louise Burdett** *and* **Catherine Denham**. **Marie Louise** *stares at an unnoticing* **Catherine** *for some time before she speaks to her. She is holding a T-shirt. Holds it away from herself. Looks at it through light.*

**Marie Louise**   What do you think?

**Catherine**   I think it suits you.

**Marie Louise** (*looking away*)   I'm not sure.

**Catherine**   It's very simple. In a good way. Not, y'know, not flashy.

**Marie Louise**   No.

**Catherine**   I think it's really smart.

*Long pause.* **Catherine** *turns from her.*

**Marie Louise**   I hate this. All . . . this.

**Catherine**   Yeah.

**Marie Louise**   Do you know what I mean?

**Catherine**   Yes.

*Very long pause.* **Catherine** *turns to watch her.*

**Marie Louise** (*about another T-shirt*)   But this I like.

**Catherine**   Oh yes.

**Marie Louise**   This is very good.

**Marie Louise** *smells the T-shirt.*

**Catherine**   It works.

**Marie Louise**   I'm sorry?

**Catherine**    I said it works. I don't think you should look further. It works.

**Marie Louise**    How much is it?

**Catherine**    I've no idea.

**Marie Louise**    Can't you look it up?

**Catherine**    I'm sorry?

**Marie Louise**    Can't you look it up? Don't you have a, a, a, a, a book or something? A book you could look the price up in?

**Catherine**    I don't work here.

**Marie Louise**    I'm sorry?

**Catherine**    I said I don't work here. I'm just, I'm looking for clothes too. I don't actually, this isn't my job.

**Marie Louise**    Oh my God. I'm so sorry. That's God, that's, that's, that's, that's –

**Catherine**    It's all right.

**Marie Louise**    No. That's terrible. How embarrassing. I honestly didn't think. I mean I thought. I wasn't thinking. Clearly. I mean clearly. Well. Where is everybody?

**Catherine**    I don't know.

**Marie Louise**    There's nobody here.

**Catherine**    I know.

**Marie Louise**    I could just walk out with this.

**Catherine**    Are you crying?

**Marie Louise**    What?

**Catherine**    Don't cry. It's all right.

**Marie Louise**    I'm not crying! For God's sake!

*She examines the garment.*

I don't even think there's, is there a little, one of those, is there a tag or anything? A magnetic strip or anything? I don't think there is. I could just walk out of the door and take this and nobody would know. There aren't any even any cameras even. These shops. I mean. These shops. Sometimes, do you ever get the feeling? You come in here. Come into one of these places and you want to be sick.

**Catherine**   I'm not sure.

**Marie Louise** (*turning to* **Catherine**)   I wanted something to wear so that if I went out I could run. Just go out and run. And now there isn't even a girl here.

**Catherine**   Maybe you should take it.

**Marie Louise**   To take my money or or or or or anything.

**Catherine**   Maybe you should.

**Marie Louise**   What?

**Catherine**   Just take it.

**Marie Louise**   I couldn't. It would just –

*She stops and stares at* **Catherine**.

**Catherine** (*staring back at her, seriously*)   I think you should.


**Dr Anne Schults***'s garden in west Camden. Afternoon.* **DI Gary Burroughs** *and* **Dr Anne Schults**. *Drinking cups of coffee. She looks at him intently.*

**Anne**   Do you miss her?

**Gary**   I'd like to see her more often, yeah.

**Anne**   Why don't you?

**Gary**   It's not always easy.

**Anne**   Do you see your parents ever?

**Gary**   I see my mum from time to time. My dad died when I was a kid.

**Anne**   How old?

**Gary** (*turning to her*)   How . . . ?

**Anne**   How old were you when your dad died?

**Gary**   Thirteen.

**Anne**   I'm sorry.

**Gary**   That's all right. It was, yer know, yer kind of don't get it, do you? (*He finishes his coffee.*) I should –

**Anne**   Do you ever get back home?

**Gary**   Not, no. No.

*He tries to put the coffee cup down. Can't find anywhere to put it.*

**Anne**   Funny, isn't it?

**Gary**   What?

**Anne**   The way people grow.

**Gary** (*moving to stand*)   I –

**Anne**   What do you think about?

**Gary**   I'm sorry?

**Anne**   When you close your eyes and you think about your home, what do you think about?

*He looks at her before he answers and then sits.*

**Gary**   Listen, Dr Schults –

**Anne**   Anne.

**Gary**   Yes –

**Anne**   Where did you go on holiday?

**Gary**   Where –

**Anne**   When you were a child, where did you go?

**Gary** (*smiling at her*)   We used to go to Peel. On the Isle of Man.

**Anne**   Did you enjoy it?

**Gary**   I loved it. Yeah.

**Anne**   Do you ever go back?

**Gary**   Not for years.

**Anne**   You should.

*Pause. He looks up. She watches him. He taps his coffee cup in the palm of his hand.*

**Gary**   I sometimes think it would be good to move there. Take Jenny.

*Very long pause. She smiles at him. Looks away smiling.*

I should be going.

**Anne**   Do you think I should go back to work?

**Gary**   It's up to you.

**Anne**   Is there a, a, a common, a common protocol about when it's wise for people to go back to work in circumstances like this?

**Gary**   Not really. No.

**Anne**   It gives me a tremendous sense of power and of importance and of worth.

**Gary**   That sounds –

**Anne**   It's been four days, Gary.

**Gary**   Yes.

**Anne** *looks away from him.*

**Anne**   I think you're very professional.

**Gary**   Thank you.

**Anne**   You seem quite compassionate.

**Gary**   I don't –

**Anne** (*looking back at him*)   Don't go.

*Silence.*

My husband can barely speak. I want him to.

*Pause.*

Every day she changes. Grows.

*Pause.*

The idea that she is in pain. Or, or, or, or crying even.

*Pause.*


*A car parked outside a house in Hackney. Afternoon.* **Gary Burroughs** *and* **Robert Evans** *watch the house.* **Gary** *is eating a burger wrapped in paper. He has a mouth full of food. Some time.*

**Robert**   How long do you think we'll be here?

**Gary**   Yer can never tell.

*Long pause.* **Robert** *looks over to* **Gary**. *He thinks about lighting a cigarette. Is interrupted.*

**Gary**   You got family up there still?

**Robert**   Mum and Dad are up there. Still where I was born. Same house. My brother moved just down the road.

**Gary**   How old's he?

**Robert**   Twenty-two. Two years younger than me.

**Gary** (*half looks at him*)   You twenty-four?

**Robert**   Yeah.

**Gary**   Really?

**Robert**   Yeah.

**Gary**    Yer don't look twenty-four.

**Robert**    Don't I?

**Gary**    No.

**Robert**    How old do I look?

**Gary** (*very definite*)    Twenty-one.

*Pause.*

**Robert**    Fuck off.

**Gary**    How do you get on with him, your brother?

**Robert** (*tapping his unlit cigarette on its packet*)    He's all right. He's a bit of a mummy's boy. Always, he was always the centre of attention with everything.

**Gary**    I see.

**Robert** (*turning to* **Gary**)    Is it always like this?

**Gary** (*staring at the house*)    Not always.

**Robert**    How long has it been now?

**Gary** (*not checking*)    Two hours. Keep watching.

**Robert** (*looking back*)    He wouldn't really have gone, would he?

**Gary**    It would be unusual. But not, completely, you know, impossible.

**Gary** *yawns in the car seat. He stretches, cramping* **Robert**.

**Robert**    Makes me sick.

**Gary**    What?

**Robert**    Thinking about it.

**Gary**    Yeah. That doesn't go.

*Beat.*

**Robert**    Does she not want Family Liaison?

**Gary**   No.

**Robert**   How come?

**Gary**   What do you mean? Not everybody does, Robert.

**Robert**   Why not?

**Gary**   Why do yer think?

**Robert**   It just means we end up doing the liaison, doing surveillance, doing paperwork, doing everything.

**Gary** (*looking at him first; some time*)   I'm not even gonna answer that.

*Some more time.*

**Robert**   I love it down here. Better than up there.

**Gary**   Got a good place?

**Robert**   Yeah. Nice. Small but, you know.

**Gary** (*finishing his burger*)   Whereabouts?

**Robert**   Up East Finchley.

**Gary**   You living on your own?

**Robert**   No. No. My girlfriend came down with me.

**Gary**   Oh yeah?

**Robert**   Esther.

**Gary**   What's she like?

**Robert**   She's . . . You know? She's very blonde. She's, I sometimes think she's quite naive. And she keeps telling me stuff. To do stuff. And getting worried about the prices of things, but she's all right.

**Gary** (*licking ketchup off his thumbs*)   She the one, you think?

**Robert**   The what?

**Gary**   The one. The big one. For you.

**Robert**    Fuck off.

**Gary**    No?

**Robert** (*looking to* **Gary**)    I don't know. You never know, do you?

**Gary**    You never do.

**Robert**    You married?

**Gary**    I am. Keep watching.

*Silence.* **Robert** *lights his cigarette.* **Gary** *looks for somewhere to put his burger paper. Finds nowhere. Puts it on the back seat.* **Gary** *looks at* **Robert**.

**Gary**    You want another coffee?

**Robert**    Yeah. Thank you.

**Gary**    There's something I wanted to tell you.

**Robert**    Oh yeah?

**Gary**    Wait here.

**Gary** *leaves* **Robert** *alone. Seventeen seconds. Comes back with two cups of coffee.*

**Robert**    This is a shit street, isn't it?

**Gary**    What?

**Robert**    Shit houses. Shit shops. Shit cars. Shit fucking people.

**Gary**    Robert.

**Robert**    Yeah.

**Gary**    I wanted to tell you.

**Robert**    What?

**Gary**    You're doing all right.

**Robert**    What?

**Gary**   You. You can calm down. You're doing fine.

**Robert**   You what?

**Gary**   You don't need to worry so much.

**Robert**   I wasn't worrying.

**Gary**   Good. (*He smiles at him.*) I was twenty.

**Robert**   Twenty.

**Gary**   Yeah.

*Some time.* **Robert** *looks at him.*

**Robert**   You still enjoy it?

**Gary**   Enjoy it?

**Robert**   This.

**Gary**   I don't know.

**Robert**   You love it, I bet.

**Gary**   I wish I didn't have to do it.

**Gary** *looks at him and so* **Robert** *returns to watching the house.*
**Gary** *watches too.*

**Robert**   You never. You'd go crazy.

**Gary**   Live by the seaside.

**Robert**   Yeah?

**Gary**   Go to live on the Isle of Man.

**Robert**   Yeah?

**Gary**   I'd love that.

*Pause.* **Robert** *springs up. Puts out his cigarette.*

**Robert**   Is that him?

**Gary**   What?

**Robert**   There!

**Gary**  Where?

**Robert**  Up there!

**Gary**  Yeah. That's him.

**Robert**  Let's go.

**Gary** (*holding his arm back*)  Just. Wait.


**Marie Louise Burdett**'s *flat. Evening.* **Marie Louise** *and* **Robert**. *He has arrived to interview her.*

**Marie Louise**  Are you?

**Robert**  Miss Burdett? I'm Detective Constable Robert Evans. Can I come in?

**Marie Louise**  I've been waiting all morning.

**Robert**  I gather you have some information regarding the search for Daisy Schults.

**Marie Louise**  They rang me first thing. Told me you'd be coming round.

**Robert**  Thank you for getting in touch.

**Marie Louise**  I wasn't sure that it was relevant.

**Robert**  Every call, Miss Burdett, I'm sure you understand, is highly appreciated.

**Marie Louise**  Yes. Yes. Yes. Yes. Can I get you something to drink or . . . ?

**Robert**  I'm fine. No. Thank you. Miss Burdett, there is a series of questions I need to ask you before I can take your statement.

**Marie Louise**  Yes. Of course.

*He pulls a notebook out of his pocket. Is just about to start writing.*

I've been so scared.

**Robert**   I'm sorry?

**Marie Louise**   No. I'm sorry. I'm being . . . (*Pause.*) I'm making myself some tea, some iced tea. Are you sure you wouldn't like some?

**Robert**   Maybe just a coffee. If that's not inconvenient.

**Marie Louise**   Fine, no, no, no, of course.

*She makes coffee and tea. He pulls a pen out of his pocket. He waits, watches her. He checks out her flat. Clocks the furniture. Maybe touches things. She talks as she prepares their drinks. He doesn't look at her while she talks.*

I've been watching the television all week. It's terrible.

**Robert**   Yes. It is.

**Marie Louise**   Makes you think.

*Gives him his drink. Takes hers. Sits. He remains standing.*

I've been here, been living here, on my own, in this flat, for what, for three months. It's too big is one thing. The flat is too big. It just, well, it is, it is, it . . .

**Robert**   It's very smart.

**Marie Louise**   Thank you.

*They smile at each other.*

I'm going to hire out one of the rooms. I think. Find somebody. I think I know who I'm going to ask. I don't want to advertise.

**Robert**   No.

**Marie Louise**   I hear noises. In the night-time. Sometimes it sounds like it's people inside my room. It can't be, can it?

**Robert**   I don't –

**Marie Louise**   I saw her photograph. They showed it on the news. At the weekend, I was watching the news. And they showed her photograph.

**Robert**   Yes.

**Marie Louise**   It's been five days now, hasn't it?

**Robert**   Four.

**Marie Louise**   I'm sorry. I'm actually finding this quite difficult.

**Robert**   That's fine. That's very common.

**Marie Louise**   How old is she?

**Robert**   She's eleven years old.

**Marie Louise**   She looks younger than that.

**Robert**   Yes.

**Marie Louise**   I saw her. Two nights ago.

*He stares at her. Puts down his coffee cup. She won't shake his gaze.*


*Panatica's cafe, Camden. Night.* **Catherine** *is clearing up.* **Gary** *is chatting to her while she works. Drinking a bottle of beer. While she talks,* **Catherine** *works, wiping tables, collecting cups, saucers, bottles, plates, glasses, waste. Returning them to her counter.* **Gary** *watches her throughout.*

**Catherine**   We used to talk about everything.

**Gary**   Yeah?

**Catherine**   You could, we could just tell each other. Tell what each other was thinking half the time.

**Gary**   That's good.

**Catherine**   It was. Yeah. It was good. (*Beat.*) What about you?

**Gary**   Can I get another drink?

*She looks at him. They grin at each other.*

Go on.

**Catherine** (*smiling, going back to work*)   Till's off.

**Gary**   Just leave it in the drawer.

**Catherine**   I can't. He'd kill us.

**Gary**   Who?

**Catherine**   Fat twat.

**Gary**   He wouldn't.

**Catherine**   You don't know him.

**Gary**   He's not so bad.

**Catherine**   You have no idea.

*Pause.* **Gary** *drains his bottle.*

**Catherine**   How was work?

**Gary** *smiles at her.*

**Gary**   It passed.

**Catherine**   You always say that.

**Gary**   Say what?

**Catherine**   Never tell us anything. I always ask you how work was and you never tell us anything about it.

**Gary**   It's not that interesting.

**Catherine**   I think it is.

**Gary**   Most of the day today I spent sitting in a car in Hackney.

**Catherine**   Why?

**Gary**   Waiting for this guy to come back home.

**Catherine**   And did he?

**Gary**   Eventually.

**Catherine**   What had he done?

**Gary** (*goes to drink and realises his bottle is empty*)   You don't want to know.

**Catherine**   Yeah I do. Tell us.

**Gary** (*swings round on his chair to look back at her*)   How was college?

**Catherine**   Spoilsport.

**Gary**   How was college?

**Catherine**   It was good.

**Gary**   What were you doing?

**Catherine**   Lectures.

**Gary**   What about?

**Catherine**   Shakespeare.

**Gary**   I used to love Shakespeare. Get us a beer.

*The tables cleared,* **Catherine** *moves back behind her counter and starts cashing the till. Putting coins and notes into separate bags. Counting the money.*

**Catherine**   No.

**Gary**   I was shit at school.

**Catherine**   Were you?

**Gary**   Spent all my time fighting and having sex.

**Catherine**   Fuck off.

**Gary**   It's true. Nearly got expelled when I was fifteen.

**Catherine**   I don't believe you.

**Gary**   How's the flat-hunting?

**Catherine**   Shocking.

**Gary**   Yeah?

**Catherine**   Killing me, I'm telling yer.

**Gary**   Don't let it.

**Catherine** (*stops work, looks up*)   Can I ask you something?

**Gary**   Go on.

**Catherine**   Do you like your job?

**Gary**   Sometimes.

**Catherine**   What do you like about it?

**Gary**   I quite like the car chases.

**Catherine**   Do you?

**Gary**   Watching people jumping to the side of the road. That's quite funny.

**Catherine**   Monkey.

**Gary**   I used to quite like a lot of the scrotes.

**Catherine**   Really?

**Gary**   When I was a bobby. A lot of them were quite funny. Got a good, you know, good sense of humour. Now there's not so much to like.

**Catherine**   No?

**Gary**   No. Different class of criminal. A lot . . .

**Catherine**   What?

**Gary**   I'm not gonna persuade you, am I?

**Catherine**   No.

**Gary**   I like you.

**Catherine**   You what?

**Gary**   I think you're very energetic.

**Catherine**   Energetic? Is that the best you can do?

**Gary**   But I think you should bend your rules about licensing for off-duty coppers.

**Catherine**   I'm tired.

**Gary**   I'm thirsty.

**Catherine**   There's a pub open, up Inverness Street.

**Gary**   I know.

**Catherine**   Go there.

**Gary**   I hate it there.

**Catherine**   Do you?

**Gary**   I'll give you a fiver.

**Catherine**   No.

**Gary**   I'll give you a lift home.

**Catherine**   No, Gary, I'm knackered. You should be going home anyway.

**Gary**   I know.

**Catherine**   Should go and see your wife.

**Gary**   I know.

**Catherine**   So go.

**Gary**   I will.

**Catherine**   Now.

**Gary**   OK.

**Catherine**   I'll see you tomorrow.

**Gary**   You really wanna know what I did today?

**Catherine**   Yeah.

**Gary**   If I tell you will you get us another beer?

**Catherine**   Depends what it is.

**Gary**   Will you?

**Catherine**   Try us.

**Gary**   All right. This is what happened to me today:


**Marie Louise** *addresses the audience.*

**Marie Louise**   So I'm coming home and I'm walking down the side of the theatre where, where, where *Les Misérables* is playing.

It's maybe eight o'clock at night.

There are people coming home from work, I guess. And other people. Going out. Going out to the theatre. Or the cinema. Or out eating in Chinatown, maybe. Men with taxis. And just by the actual theatre, by the doors at the back, there's a five-year-old child on her own. But it's too dark. It's late. She's too vulnerable to be out here on her own. She can't be. But actually I think she is.

Just near there I see a younger boy holding hands with his mother. He's got this soft blond hair and he's very excited. Stamping his feet up and down like a robot or something. And there are these lights on his trainers which I think, I just think is fantastic.

And down, off, I don't know, Old Compton Street maybe, or one of the streets there, coming up to it I hear the sound of a girl and she's actually, what she's doing is she's screaming. And that seems horrible. But when I get to the alleyway where she is, I see her. She's the same age as the first girl. But what she's doing is she's screaming, just so that she can listen to the sound of the scream reflected on the walls in the alley. Which looks quite fun to me. I almost want to scream too. With her. And everywhere I look I notice all the children. There just seems to be. It's like there are children everywhere.

I get on to Oxford Street, heading up to Oxford Circus and before I get there I, this is a bit naughty, I decide that I'm going to go into Thornton's, there. I really want to buy some toffee. I just have this this this this urge. So I've decided, really decided, that I'm going to have this toffee. But in the shop, I get there and in the shop they only have diabetic toffee. That's all they have. In the whole shop! So I buy some. And I eat the whole packet. So that I start to feel a bit sick. And when I come out it's like all the children have gone. They've just disappeared. Where can they all of gone? Just like that. It doesn't make any sense. But. I can't see *any*.

I go into Top Shop. I don't buy anything.

And walk past and look up at that church there. In fact, it's not a church, is it? It's a monument.

*Beat.*

*Blackout. Ten seconds.*


**April**

*Kentish Town police station.* **Gary Burroughs**'s *office. Morning.* **Gary** *and* **Robert** *are working through catalogues of photofit photographs.* **Robert** *pauses in his work. Looks up at* **Gary**. **Gary** *keeps working throughout.*

**Robert**    Nothing?

**Gary** (*still searching*)    Nothing.

**Robert**    Maybe . . .

**Gary**    What?

**Robert**    Her description was very specific, but . . . .

**Gary** (*trying not to look up from his work*)    But what?

**Robert**    Maybe she was just wrong.

**Gary**    –

**Robert**   Maybe she was just fucking cracking up.

**Gary**   –

**Robert**   If she was . . . ?

**Gary** (*looking up briefly*)   Yeah?

**Robert**   Then what have we got?

**Gary**   Not much.

**Robert**   No.

*They continue working.*

How's Dr Schults?

**Gary** (*turning a page*)   Bearing up.

**Robert**   Yeah?

**Gary** *reaches up to get a cigarette without ever letting his eyes leave the page. Has to feel for the cigarette with his fingers.*

**Gary**   She's very clear-headed. She seems quite . . .

**Robert**   What?

**Gary**   She talks a lot of sense.

**Robert**   Well, she's a teacher, Gary. I should hope she talks a lot of sense.

**Gary**   I quite like her.

**Robert**   Oh yeah?

**Gary**   Not . . . Fucking dick.

**Gary** *lights his cigarette.*

**Robert**   How was he this week?

**Gary**   Quiet.

**Robert**   Quiet how?

**Gary**   He cried.

**Robert**   Right.

**Gary** (*looking up*)   Are you looking?

**Robert** (*looking down to photos*)   Course.

**Gary**   Because if we miss one, Robert . . .

**Robert**   We won't.

**Gary** *clears his throat. Turns another page.*

**Robert**   Our kid's coming down.

**Gary**   Yeah?

**Robert**   Going up Centre Point tonight. Play a bit of pool. Should come with us.

**Gary**   You what?

**Robert**   Should do.

**Gary**   –

**Robert**   I'll be glad just to get out of the house.

**Gary**   –

**Robert**   Fucking Esther.

**Gary**   –

**Robert**   I said, 'Fucking Esther.'

**Gary**   What?

**Robert**   Doing my head in a bit.

**Gary**   I see.

**Robert**   She hates it here.

**Gary**   Does she?

**Robert**   Keeps going on. Fucking . . . *All* the *time*. About getting stabbed. Getting robbed. Fucking Asian boys on the estate robbing her.

**Gary**   Did they?

**Robert**   No.

**Gary**   –

**Robert**   Worse back home. Fucking Pakis back home fucking just –

**Gary** (*looks straight at him*)   Don't.

**Robert** (*looks straight back*)   What?

**Gary**   Just don't. Just shut it.

**Robert**   Just a word. Just a word, Gary.

*Pause. They work in silence for a while.*

**Gary**   How you getting on?

**Robert**   Nowt.

**Gary**   If we don't find anything, you know what they'll do, don't you?

**Robert**   Yeah.

**Gary**   So find something.

*Pause.* **Gary** *turns another page. Turns it back. Checks a photo and turns the page again.*

**Robert**   How's Jenny?

**Gary**   She's all right, thank you.

**Robert**   Could bring her with yer.

**Gary**   What?

**Robert**   If you come out tonight.

**Gary**   Maybe.

**Robert**   I'd like to meet her.

**Gary**   Yeah?

**Robert**   You never fancied kids?

**Gary** (*looking up*)   You what?

**Robert**   I was just wondering if you and Jenny, why you, you know, never had children or owt.

**Gary** *looks at him for three seconds.*

**Robert**   Esther's started asking. Reckons it'd be good. Reckons it'd be all right. I don't know what I'd do if she got pregnant. See all this. Wouldn't want to inflict this on anybody. It's not, not, not, just not fair.

**Gary**   Too expensive.

**Robert**   Yeah?

**Gary**   Oh yeah.

*Some time.* **Robert** *picks up and examines a witness statement, visibly a piece of text rather than a photograph.*

**Robert** (*savouring the name*)   Marie Louise Burdett. When I went round to her flat. You know those big flats up Kentish Town. The way she looked at us.

**Gary**   –

**Robert**   It was weird. Looking at her. Trying to listen to her. Half thinking I want to fuck you.

**Gary** (*looks up*)   Shouldn't do that.

**Robert**   What?

**Gary**   Shouldn't talk about people like that.

**Robert**   Yer saying you never?

**Gary**   How old are you again?

*Beat.* **Gary** *picks up the statement.* **Robert** *rests his feet on the table.* **Gary** *freezes.*

**Robert**   You found anything?

**Gary**   No I haven't.

**Robert**   It's hopeless, Gary. Isn't it?

**Gary**   What?

**Robert**   Ten weeks it's been now.

**Gary** *moves away from him.*

**Robert**   What are you gonna do?

**Gary**   I have no idea.

**Robert**   You gonna come out with us?

**Gary**   What?

**Robert**   Tonight, Gary. You coming or what?


**Marie Louise** *and* **Catherine** *are in a public square in Islington. Lunchtime.* **Catherine** *lies on the ground looking up.* **Marie Louise** *sits on the bench. They are playing a game.*

**Marie Louise**   In Bloomsbury.

**Catherine**   Bloomsbury?!?

**Marie Louise** (*embarrassed*)   Yeah.

**Catherine**   Wow.

**Marie Louise**   What?

**Catherine**   When?

**Marie Louise**   Nineteen seventy-five.

**Catherine**   So you're twenty-seven.

**Marie Louise** (*simultaneously*)   Twenty-six . . . seven. Shit.

**Catherine**   I'm nineteen eighty-one. You're six years older than me. (*Beat.*) I have to tell you something.

**Marie Louise**   What?

**Catherine**   I . . . It can wait.

*Short time.*

What was your school like?

**Marie Louise**   It was. You know, I don't really remember that much about it.

**Catherine**   No?

**Marie Louise**   I remember the boys in the year above me.

**Catherine**   What were they like?

**Marie Louise**   I thought they were gorgeous. (*Long pause.*) What about you?

**Catherine**   I remember my friend Lucy, all her toys, how they were better than mine. And I remember going round to her house and eating peanuts and ice cream. And the smell of grass at school. And I had this Barbie doll with this metallic dress that was the coolest thing I ever saw.

*Short time.*

I can't stop thinking about that girl.

**Marie Louise**   No.

**Catherine**   How long has it been now?

**Marie Louise**   Three months.

**Catherine**   Last week, I just went out, I bought a coat. A hundred-pound coat. Just to get my mind . . . I don't have a hundred pounds.

**Marie Louise**   No.

*They spend some time soaking in the sun. Then* **Catherine** *props herself up on her elbows. Looks up at* **Marie Louise**.

**Catherine**   This is good.

**Marie Louise**   What?

**Catherine**   This. It's nice.

**Marie Louise**   Yes. It is.

**Catherine**   We should do this more often.

**Marie Louise**   We should.

**Catherine** (*sitting up*)   What was your mum like?

**Marie Louise**   She was very beautiful.

**Catherine**   I bet she was.

**Marie Louise**   Why?

**Catherine**   Because I think you are too.

**Marie Louise**   She used to be a model. And a painter.

**Catherine**   Did she?

**Marie Louise**   She sat, actually, one time, this is the truth, she sat for David Hockney.

**Catherine**   What about your dad?

**Marie Louise**   He's . . . He's always wringing his hands. I hate that.

**Catherine** (*going to sit with her*)   And do you prefer cats or dogs?

**Marie Louise**   Cats.

**Catherine**   And what's your favourite clothing?

**Marie Louise**   Anything cashmere.

**Catherine**   Get you!

**Marie Louise**   What!?!

**Catherine**   What kind of music do you like?

**Marie Louise**   Jazz. Jazzy. Jazz music.

**Catherine** (*looking straight at her*)   And have you ever been in love?

**Marie Louise** (*looking out*)   Yes.

**Catherine**   Have you?

**Marie Louise**   Yes.

**Catherine**   Who with?

**Marie Louise**   With my last boyfriend.

**Catherine**   What was he called?

**Marie Louise**   Steven.

**Catherine** (*pushing herself forward with the balls of both hands*)
And what happened to Steven?

**Marie Louise**   It didn't work out.

**Catherine**   Why?

**Marie Louise**   'Cause he was just –

**Catherine**   What?

**Marie Louise**   Nothing.

*Silence.* **Catherine** *looks out too.*

**Marie Louise**   I want my mum to leave my dad.

*Silence.*

Actually I want him to die.

*They laugh together. Pause.*

**Catherine**   I love my parents, me. (*Beat.*) Marie Louise.

**Marie Louise** (*turns to her*)   Do you want kids?

**Catherine**   You what?

**Marie Louise**   Do you, Catherine?

**Catherine**   Yes.

**Marie Louise**   Do you?

**Catherine**   Definitely.

**Marie Louise**   I think you'd be a good mother.

**Catherine**   I think I'd be a GREAT mother. Yeah. (*Beat.*)
Marie Louise.

**Marie Louise**   I think you're . . .

**Catherine**   What?

**Marie Louise**   You're very, stylish. You have a great style.

**Catherine**   I want to tell you something.

**Marie Louise**   Do you know what frightens me?

**Catherine**   What?

**Marie Louise**   You'll think I'm very strange.

**Catherine**   What?

**Marie Louise**   I'm frightened that I'm going to live too long.

*Long pause.*

What was it that you wanted to tell me?

**Catherine**   Marie Louise, I can't pay my rent this month.


*Panatica's cafe. Afternoon.* **Gary** *is drinking coffee. He is on his feet. Pacing.* **Catherine** *is working. She is pouring salt from a large bottle into individual table salt cellars. He doesn't look at her when he talks to her. Looks out of the windows, out of the door, at the floor, into his coffee cup, anywhere but at her.*

**Gary**   You should leave.

**Catherine**   You don't know what you're talking about.

**Gary**   I do.

**Catherine**   I need the money.

**Gary**   That's a bullshit excuse.

**Catherine**   No it isn't, Gary. What is it with you today?

**Gary**   There are plenty of jobs better, more interesting, more demanding, more . . . you're just –

**Catherine**    I like it.

**Gary**    No you don't.

**Catherine**    I like the punters. I like the conversation. I like you normally. Unless you're being −

**Gary**    And what about fat twat?

**Catherine**    I hate him but −

**Gary**    You see.

**Catherine**    Everybody hates their boss.

**Gary**    I don't hate my boss.

**Catherine**    That's different.

**Gary**    Why?

**Catherine**    'Cause your job is your career.

**Gary**    My career?

**Catherine**    What you are. Your job is what you are. But this is a just a way −

**Gary**    What are you going on about?

**Catherine**    Just a way of paying for me to get myself through college. I need it. I won't be doing it for ever.

**Gary**    I just think you're worth more than this.

**Catherine**    I am. I am worth more than this.

**Gary**    I was so glad to get out. Me. Of Brum. Just go.

*Beat. He stands still. Puts his coffee down. Flexes and unflexes his fingers. Looks at her.*

Can I have a beer please?

**Catherine**    You told me not to serve you any beer.

**Gary**    I know.

**Catherine**    You told me not to.

**Gary**   I changed my mind.

**Catherine**   Have you finished work yet?

**Gary**   Yes.

**Catherine**   Have you really?

**Gary**   Yes.

**Catherine**   You haven't, have you?

**Gary**   No.

**Catherine**   It's a contravention of my licence to serve an on-duty policeman.

**Gary**   I know that! I won't *nick* you!

**Catherine**   I'll get you a coffee.

**Gary** (*moving in on her*)   I *want* a *beer*.

**Catherine**   Gary. No.

**Gary**   You think I can't . . . I've been drinking since I was thirteen. I've been smoking since I was eleven.

**Catherine**   What's that got to do with anything?

**Gary** (*raising his fist above the back of his head*)   It's just fucking ridiculous, Catherine, honestly, mate. It's fucking –

**Catherine**   Gary, don't talk to me like that.

**Gary**   If you knew what I had to do this afternoon!

**Catherine**   What?

*No response.*

What do you mean?

*Some time.* **Gary** *tries to calm down. Inhales and exhales through his teeth.* **Catherine** *puts the bottle away and starts screwing the tops on the cellars.* **Gary** *turns away from her again, wrestles with the change in his pockets.*

**Gary**   How's your new house?

**Catherine**    Arright.

**Gary**    And the new flatmate?

**Catherine**    She's arright. Bit.

**Gary**    What?

**Catherine**    She's very as mad as a fucking hat. But she's all right. Harmless, you know? Rent's cheap.

**Gary** (*slight laugh*)    That's good.

**Catherine**    Croydon's just the same, you know.

**Gary**    What?

**Catherine** (*while she talks,* **Gary** *nods*)    No different to Birmingham. Just shit. Everything. Hate it. Better up here.

**Gary** (*turns to look at her*)    You think so?

**Catherine**    At least there's things to do.

**Gary**    Yeah.

*Beat. They look at each other.*


**Robert** *addresses the audience.*

**Robert**    I leave my house and I'm heading for the tube.

It's dark.

I can hear some music coming from somewhere behind me and to my left.

I'm aware that I'm walking much slower than I ordinarily would have done.

And I turn the corner, change direction and the music seems to be still coming from behind me. Still to me left. And and and I'm counting the uncracked paving stones. And there seems to be just hundreds of them.

Underneath the railway tracks at Kentish Town West a train goes past and I just think, how much I want to be asleep on a train. How good that would feel. Actually. Right now.

And the light is dimming.

And it's getting cold.

And just turning before Kentish Town Road, there's a park, a kiddies' playground, bits of grass, all that and there is litter, strewn all over it. Cans and waste paper and sweet wrappers and bottles. And it seems, to me, it seems just plain shameful. That people should do that. They should concrete the lot. I mean, why bother? They should just cover it up.

West of Kentish Town Road there are cranes putting together a block of flats or offices or something. I love the way that cranes look in the nights. Like birds. Like huge spiders. And I want to, just to climb up it. Nobody would see us. Nobody would stop us. Nobody would do owt. And the things you could see. It would be just magnificent.

And the music's getting louder which doesn't make sense. But I can't quite distinguish it. And it's still coming from behind me and still coming from the left.

I turn up the main road heading towards the pedestrian crossing and for the first time I remember where I am. Exactly where I am. And there's the yellow and the red and the light of McDonald's and I'm so happy to see it. To know that it is there. That it remains there. It looks like a beacon. Like a big old glow. And I cross the pedestrian crossing. And I'm in the tube station. With the floor wet and cold and the wind and the noise and the smell of a tube station, the smell that tube stations always have. And I go straight down.

*Kentish Town police station.* **Gary Burroughs**'s *office. Early evening.* **Marie Louise** *sits with her hands folded on her lap.*

**Gary** *sits opposite her. He has a pen in his hand, a folder open in front of him.*

**Marie Louise**    I don't believe this. I don't believe that nothing has been, can be, has been done.

**Gary**    Miss Burdett. There are some details I need to check.

**Marie Louise**    I really. I don't. Can I speak to your supervising officer please?

**Gary**    I need to clarify some of the things which you told my colleague.

**Marie Louise**    It's been months and months. You're doing nothing.

**Gary**    There are some elements of your statement you might wish to clarify.

**Marie Louise**    To *clarify*? I'd like to speak to your supervising officer please.

**Gary**    That may not be necessary. You told my colleague DC Evans that you saw a girl that you thought resembled Daisy Schults in the Seven Dials area of Covent Garden two days prior to your interview on the 23rd of January this year, is that correct?

**Marie Louise**    I think so.

**Gary**    You think so?

**Marie Louise**    Yes it is. It is correct.

**Gary**    That she was wearing a red coat. That her hair was tied back. These were details that you recognised from the family photograph broadcast shortly before you contacted the police. That you were surprised because she seemed to be in a state of some distress and that she was being forced north across the Seven Dials by a man that you describe as being a black-haired Caucasian aged perhaps forty, slightly overweight. Is *that* correct?

**Marie Louise**   That's correct. That's all correct.

**Gary**   This is the statement that you are intent on pursuing?

**Marie Louise**   I want to know why nothing has been done about what I saw.

**Gary**   You claim, and I quote from your statement: 'Two nights ago. Maybe about six o'clock.' And then when asked why you didn't contact the police immediately, you said, and again I quote: 'I waited a day to be sure it was her.'

**Marie Louise**   Yes.

**Gary**   Miss Burdett. That would have timed your sighting of her at six o'clock on Sunday the 21st.

**Marie Louise**   This is absurd.

**Gary**   The photograph wasn't broadcast until the ten o'clock news, Miss Burdett.

**Marie Louise**   –

**Gary**   You couldn't have seen the photograph before the time you saw the girl that you recognised as Daisy, Miss Burdett. Nobody could have done.

**Marie Louise**   –

**Gary**   You know it wasn't her, don't you, Miss Burdett?

**Marie Louise**   I might have got the time wrong.

**Gary**   You were clear and specific at the time of your interview.

**Marie Louise**   I might have done. People make mistakes.

**Gary**   When you were questioned you repeated the same details over, on two occasions.

*Pause.* **Gary** *looks at her. She looks away.*

**Marie Louise**   Can I have a glass of water please?

**Gary**   It happens all the time. People see, they think they
see things. They want to see things. It's like they see
phantoms of –

**Marie Louise**   It wasn't a phantom.

**Gary**   We don't charge them normally. We could.
Wasting police time.

**Marie Louise**   I saw her.

**Gary**   Miss Burdett, we decided not to pursue this line of
inquiry.

*Pause.* **Gary** *gathers papers.*

**Marie Louise**   I don't know what to say.

**Gary** (*standing*)   Thank you for your concern. I understand
your anxiety. It must have felt as though we were wilfully
neglecting your statement. I can assure you that wasn't the
case. I want to thank you for your time.

**Marie Louise**   I don't know what to do.

*Beat. He touches her hand.*

**Gary**   I understand, y'know? I do. People get . . .


*Late afternoon. Alone at first,* **Anne** *waits at home for the expected
arrival of* **Gary** *and* **Robert***. They arrive after a few moments.
They are wearing coats. She welcomes them.*

**Anne** (*standing*)   Hello. Hello. Come in. Come in. Just, just,
just, can I take your coats?

**Robert**   Thank you.

**Gary**   Thank you.

*They take their coats off. Remain standing. She hangs their coats up.
Comes back. Folds her arms.*

**Anne**   Please. Sit. Sit. Sit down. Just. How are you both?

**Gary**   We're all right. Yeah.

*They sit.*

**Robert**   Yeah. Fine.

**Anne**   Good. Good. That's good. That's . . . Can I get you anything? Please. A cup of tea. Or, or, or coffee.

**Gary**   We –

**Anne**   Please.

**Gary**   A coffee would be lovely.

**Robert**   Yes. For me as well.

**Anne**   Good. Coffee. How would you like it?

**Gary**   Black, no sugar.

**Robert**   Milk, one. Please.

**Anne**   Right. Good. Just. Wait here.

*She leaves them. They both sit down. Still for some time.* **Gary** *turns his mobile phone off.* **Robert** *stares at the floor.*

**Anne** (*off*)   It looks like it's going to be a beautiful day tomorrow. They said. I saw.

**Gary**   Yeah. I saw that.

**Anne** (*off*)   We, me and and and John, we might go out to the countryside, if it stays good at the weekend.

**Gary**   Oh yeah?

*She comes back in with a tray of coffee and biscuits.*

**Anne**   Go down to Sussex. Maybe Brighton. Here you are.

**Gary**   Lovely.

**Anne**   I brought you some biscuits. Have a biscuit.

**Gary** (*taking one*)   Thank you.

**Robert** (*taking one*)   Thank you.

*They put their biscuits down and don't touch them again.*

**Gary** How is Mr Petrie?

**Anne** He's all right. Yes. He's all right.

**Gary** Good (*Beat.*) Dr Schults –

**Anne** Anne.

**Gary** Anne. We've got some news.

**Anne** Right. Right. Right. Right. Right.

**Gary** Would you like to sit down?

**Anne** No no no I'll stand.

**Gary** Anne, the investigation, as you know, the investigation has been proceeding for ten weeks now.

**Anne** Yes.

**Gary** There's been no real progress.

**Anne** No.

**Gary** The description we were given matched nothing that we have on our records. It led nowhere.

**Anne** No. You said. It wasn't. Necessarily. It could have been a perfectly . . .

**Gary** Yes.

*Beat.*

At a meeting this morning a decision was made regarding the search for Daisy. It has been decided that the evidence that we have on the case does not warrant the level of manpower currently being expended in the investigation. We remain too unconfident about specific elements. The details of her activities. The details of her appearance. Her knowledge of the environment. We have found no clues. No developments have been made. At present we have ten officers working on the investigation full-time and a reserve staff of fifty officers pursuing the investigation on at least a

part-time basis. It has been decided that eight of the
remaining ten officers involved in the search for Daisy will
be moved away from working exclusively on the case and
that the fifty officers in reserve will be returned to their
regular duties. This will leave two officers involved
exclusively in her search, representing the Missing Persons
Division but working for the Child Protection Team. These
will be myself and Detective Constable Evans, Robert.

**Anne**  Right.

**Gary**  We have also decided upon a new tactic in
proceeding with the investigation. We have decided to scale
down the geographical area in which we are going to be
searching. We've decided to concentrate on a much more
thorough investigation of the north London area.

**Anne**  What do you mean?

**Gary**  We are set to embark on a very thorough and
comprehensive series of interviews with all residents of north
London currently recorded on the national register.

**Anne**  You're going to . . .

**Gary**  A series of interviews that will in time move away
from the north London area and take in all of central and
then greater London.

*Silence.*

Do you understand what I have told you?

*Silence.*

**Anne**  Doesn't it warrant more officers? Gary, if, if, if
you've found nothing. Gary. If you've found nothing then
doesn't it make more sense to employ more officers rather
than, rather than, rather than less? I mean, it sounds like
you're giving up!

**Gary**  Dr Schults, in cases like this case, sometimes a more
concentrated –

**Anne**    Hasn't the register been checked already? Gary?

**Gary**    There's a difference between an inquiry and an interview –

**Anne**    Do you think she's been taken now?

**Gary**    I'm afraid we have to consider that as a possibility.

*She looks at him for a long time.*

**Anne**    What do you *think*?

**Gary**    I don't know.

**Anne**    No, I know that but but but what do you *think*?

**Gary**    I really can't say. I just don't know.

**Anne**    And if she has been it's very likely that she's been killed, isn't it?

**Gary**    I couldn't say.

**Anne**    But she probably has been, hasn't she?

**Gary**    I don't know.

**Anne**    She can't have been gone for for for so long. Nobody could have taken her for so long, for that, and kept her alive, could they?

**Gary**    We can't possibly tell at this stage.

**Anne**    Does that happen ever?

**Gary**    We couldn't say at this stage.

**Anne**    I'm asking you if that happens ever?

**Gary**    It's very, very unusual.

**Anne**    But it happens. It has happened.

**Gary**    Yes. It has happened.

**Anne**    Have you known it happen?

**Gary**    I –

**Anne**   Have you investigated a case in which it has happened?. Gary, have you?

*No response. He looks down.*

Oh Christ, God.

*She sits and cries. Bites her fist. Her shoulders shaking.*

**Gary**   Can I get you anything? (*To* **Robert**.) Some water.

**Robert** *fetches water.* **Gary** *stands to touch her back. Doesn't.*

**Gary**   Anne, I swear to you we will try, with everything that we have, with *everything* to find her. (*Pause.*) Is there anything which you are unclear about? Anything at all.

**Anne** (*arms wrapped around herself, looking up*)   No. No. No. I don't think so.

**Robert** *returns.*

**Gary**   There is still the option of employing a full-time family liaison officer –

**Anne**   No.

**Gary**   Anne, after we've left, this afternoon, or tonight, if you have any questions about this. About anything regarding this or about anything, ring me. You can ring me at the office or on the office mobile, or here, this is my personal mobile. Any time. Day or night. Don't even hesitate. Do you promise me?

**Anne**   I –

**Gary**   Anne.

**Anne**   Yes. I promise.

**Robert**   What time is Mr Schults coming home?

**Anne**   It's Mr Petrie. My husband's name is Petrie.

**Catherine** *addresses the audience.*

**Catherine**    I'm heading east.

Out towards the City.

There's this man on the Central Line. And when I see him
for the first time he looks quite together. But I'm drawn
back to him. To looking at him. He can't hold my eye
contact. And as I look at him I notice that his fingernails are
dusty. And that his raincoat is old and dusty too. And he is
unshaven. And his hair is cut badly. And that there are cuts
on his face.

The floor of the tube train is spattered with phlegm. And it
is men who have spat there.

There's this boy, he must be maybe thirteen years old and
he is too exhausted even to hold his head up.

And I can smell rubber and aftershave.

And when the train pulls into the station the screech of the
brakes is horrible. Horrible. And I can't believe that nobody
else notices. And I'm not sure but I think that the man I saw
on the train gets off at the same station as me.

And there is flute music in the station, echoing down the
corridors and the sound of the lift-doors-closing alarm.

In my mouth I can taste Red Bull and chocolate.

And outside on Cheapside there is a crane, towering above
me, and it's horrible. And the sound of slaughtering metal.
And the cars are being shaken by the bass tubes. And the
men inside them. Physically shaken. You can watch them.
And feel it in your feet. And the men's voices outside the
bars there are the same. They are all drinking outside in
their, in their, in their suits and their voices have, they have
the same violence.

I look round to see if he's been following me because I
sensed something, I sensed something I sensed a, a, a, a. But
there's nobody there.

And the doors on the bars look like they want to crush you.

And there are no stars in the sky.

And I can't find the moon.

*Blackout. Ten seconds.*


## August

*Night-time.* **Robert** *is drinking in the Centre Point pool hall. At the table there.* **Gary** *has found him.* **Robert** *is drunk. Holding a pool cue. He holds it like a weapon almost. There is a long pause before they speak. Looking straight at one another.* **Gary** *holds his hand up, as though warning him or calming him.*

**Robert**   Your fault this.

**Gary**   Robert.

*Pause.*

**Robert** (*breathing hard*)   Sometimes I want to kill you.

**Gary**   What?

**Robert**   Should have got him.

**Gary**   I –

**Robert**   Should have gone in. Should have done, done, done, done *something*.

**Gary**   Robert, please, keep your voice –

**Robert** (*as though straining to keep quiet*)   I wanted to and you *stopped* me. *You stopped me.* And it was wrong and you should start to think about how you are going to take responsibility for that, Gary, because it was your fault.

**Gary**   Robert, listen.

**Robert**   With your stubborn fucking patronising fucking . . .

**Robert** *raises the cue slightly.*

**Gary**  –

**Robert**  I hate it. I hate the way you fucking look at me sometimes. And the way you fucking talk to me. And talk about me. And the way you never listen to a fucking word I say but you just fucking just always just don't say nothing. I hate it.

*Pause.*

And I hate the way you eat.

**Gary**  Robert, calm –

**Robert** *looks around himself as though checking other people's reactions to his anger. He is straining to hold his voice down.*

**Robert**  Don't tell me to calm down! For fuck's sake! Coming down here! Telling me! How fucking dare you? How fucking dare you do that?

**Gary**  I had something to tell –

**Robert**  Honestly, Gary, fucking don't.

*Pause.* **Gary** *lets him settle and stew.* **Robert** *turns away, lowers his cue.*

**Robert**  This place! It's fucking crackers! It does my head in. It makes me want to just fucking –

*He becomes still.*

I go home at night and just the sound now of the way that Esther has started to breathe even makes me fucking want to tear out my teeth. And it's your fault.

*Long pause. He stares at* **Gary** *who stands still.*

**Robert**  She keeps going on.

**Gary**  Robert, something's –

**Robert**  I'm going, me. I'm gonna fuck off. Fuck off back up home. Fuck this. Fuck this job. Fucking – Fuck you. Fuck you. Fuck you. Fuck her. Fuck her kid. Fuck 'em all.

**Robert** *lets the cue drop to the floor.*

**Gary**   Robert, they've found a body.

**Robert**   They what?

**Gary**   Just heard. This evening. Some woman. On the north bank of the Thames. Low tide. Just west of Millbank. Opposite MI5. It's a little girl.

**Robert**   Right.

**Gary**   We're going in to see it first thing tomorrow.

*Long pause.* **Robert** *looks away from* **Gary** *for three seconds and then looks back at his chin.*

**Robert**   Not everybody likes you, y'know.

**Gary**   You what?

**Robert**   You think they do but you're fucking wrong. Not everybody does.

**Gary**   You swear too much. You shouldn't swear as much as you do. There's no need for it. Tomorrow morning, you better be ready.


*Panatica's cafe. Night.* **Gary** *is drinking with* **Catherine**. *Looking largely at their drinks.*

**Catherine**   You're very quiet.

**Gary**   What?

**Catherine**   Tonight.

**Gary**   Am I?

**Catherine**   Bad day?

**Gary**   No no no no. It was all right. It was, yeah. It was good. It was fine.

**Catherine**   We've been dead.

**Gary**   Yeah?

**Catherine**   Too hot to work.

**Gary**   I know that feeling.

**Catherine**   Too hot to do anything. I hate it here when it's hot.

**Gary**   How come?

**Catherine**   It gets so grimy. Sorry. I shouldn't be telling you this, should I. But it does.

**Gary**   It's all right. I don't really eat here.

**Catherine**   If you did I'd tell you not to.

**Gary**   Why?

**Catherine**   The kitchen here. Makes you sick.

**Gary**   Does it?

**Catherine**   He wants locking up. I'll tell you that for nothing. If anybody does he does. Fat cunt.

*Pause. He looks straight at her.*

**Gary**   I wish . . .

**Catherine**   What?

**Gary** *smiles, pulls a cigarette out. Doesn't light it.*

**Gary**   I like talking to you.

**Catherine**   Good.

**Gary**   I wish you didn't always just make me leave all the time.

**Catherine**   I wish you'd let me go home on time. Get some kip. Yer with me?

**Gary**   Can I ask you something?

**Catherine**   Go on.

**Gary**   Would you want to be a mother ever? If you had the chance.

**Catherine**   Damn right I would.

**Gary**   Would you?

**Catherine**   Yeah. Duurr.

**Gary**   What?

**Catherine**   Course I would.

**Gary**   That's good.

**Catherine**   I'd be a great mum, me and all.

**Gary**   Would you?

**Catherine**   Yeah.

**Gary**   How's that?

**Catherine**   What do you mean?

**Gary**   What would make you a good mum, do you think?

**Catherine**   I'd be very patient. I'd be very generous. I'd be very loving.

**Gary** *puts his cigarette in his mouth.*

**Gary**   Yeah.

**Catherine**   Yeah what?

**Gary**   I think you would. I think you're right.

**Gary** *lights a match. Lets it burn for a bit. Shakes it out. Takes his cigarette out of his mouth and puts it back in the packet.*

**Catherine**   What you asking that for?

**Gary**   Just . . .

*Pause.*

*He looks away for some time, drinks, wipes his mouth with the back of his hand and then looks straight back at her.*

Do you know something?

**Catherine**    What?

**Gary**    I think you're lovely.

*Long pause.*

People should know things like that about themselves. I think. I think not enough people tell each other things like that and they should and I wanted to tell you.

**Catherine**    Thank you.

**Gary**    I had this thing.

**Catherine**    What?

**Gary**    When I was younger, I used to go and look at galleries. Just look at pictures. Go to the National Gallery. Or the National Portrait Gallery or some of the smaller ones. I used to like looking at the pictures. Sometimes in the middle of the day when I was working I'd do it. Just go and I was thinking. I can't.

**Catherine**    What?

**Gary**    This is going to sound really stupid actually.

**Catherine**    What?

**Gary**    I would have liked to take you to one of these galleries. Go with you. Just go and look at some pictures. But I can't. It'd be. I just – There's no way.

*Long pause.*

**Catherine**    No.

**Gary**    Just . . . stupid. I'm sorry.

*Morning. Harvey Nichols. The cafe in the food hall on the fifth floor. A beautiful new morning. Big, big presence of sunshine.* **Marie Louise** *and* **Catherine**. *Long pause.* **Marie Louise** *looks out of the window. And then looks straight at* **Catherine**.

**Marie Louise**   I wanted to ask you something.

**Catherine**   What?

**Marie Louise**   I might not though.

**Catherine**   What?

**Marie Louise**   No. I think I won't.

**Catherine**   What?

**Marie Louise**   It's so bright! God!

**Catherine**   –

**Marie Louise**   You know you said you really want to have a baby.

**Catherine**   Yeah.

**Marie Louise**   I've been thinking about this all morning. Since they found that girl. And what I thought was that actually, I'm terrified of babies. I am. They, they, they, they scare me.

**Catherine**   It must have been –

**Marie Louise**   Just the feeling of them.

**Catherine**   Don't you –

**Marie Louise** (*looking out, maybe shading her eyes*)   I like it here. I think this view is my favourite view over the city. The gardens. All of the high street.

**Catherine**   Good hot chocolate.

**Marie Louise** (*looking back briefly*)   Good what?

**Catherine**   This hot chocolate. It's very chocolatey. Very thick.

**Marie Louise**   It's such a beautiful morning.

**Catherine**   Yeah.

**Marie Louise**   I love summer in England. A really good summer's day. You don't get them very often.

*Long pause.* **Catherine** *stirs her hot chocolate. The spoon rattling around the sides of the cup. She goes to raise it to her mouth.*

**Marie Louise** (*looking back*)   Do you miss having a man around?

**Catherine**   No.

**Marie Louise**   No, me neither.

**Catherine**   I should hope not.

**Marie Louise**   I think I'm doing fine. I think it's great. It's good. I like it. Better off without them.

*Pause.*

Have you ever done anything stupid? I mean really stupid and terrible.

**Catherine**   –

**Marie Louise**   One time I told something to the police and it wasn't true. Is that, do you think that's awful?

**Catherine**   It depends what –

**Marie Louise**   I thought, I really thought that I saw this thing once. (*Beat.*) Just a child, she was, just, smiling. And now I don't think that I did.

*Beat.* **Catherine** *stares at her.* **Marie Louise** *looks away.*

**Catherine**   Marie Louise –

**Marie Louise**   There are so many things I'm going to do this next six months. Before the end of the year . . .

**Catherine**   What like?

**Marie Louise**   I'm going to sing.

**Catherine**   You sing all the time.

**Marie Louise**   No, but really sing. Take it seriously.

**Catherine**   I think that's –

**Marie Louise**   And I'm going to start writing.

**Catherine**   Writing?

**Marie Louise**   Just writing things down. Maybe try to send some things in somewhere. It's all about –

**Catherine**   What?

**Marie Louise**   Indelibility. To indelibly leave my thumbprint. So that it's like you're not even dead. Should we get a cat?

**Catherine**   A cat.

**Marie Louise**   I always wanted to get a cat but I don't think we should now. Catherine, I heard what you did.

**Catherine**   What?

**Marie Louise**   I heard what you did to me.

**Catherine**   What?

**Marie Louise**   Just. Don't.

**Catherine**   Marie Louise, I don't know what you're talking about.

**Marie Louise**   Sometimes I want to get all my hair and just cut it all off. Do you ever get like that?

**Catherine**   Sometimes.

**Marie Louise**   And and and washing up! Because let's face it. With you. I could just open the window, yeah, and just throw them all away and buy a whole new big load of plates.

**Catherine**   Have I done something to upset you, Marie Louise –

**Marie Louise**   To 'upset' me?

**Catherine**   Because if I have –

**Marie Louise**    No, not 'upset'. Not 'upset'.

**Catherine**    I really don't know what it is and I –

**Marie Louise**    Let's just not. Talk about it. It's better not to. It's just something I heard. Might not even be true.

**Catherine**    If you'd tell me.

**Marie Louise**    I have had such a . . . I didn't sleep.

**Catherine**    –

**Marie Louise**    I can't stop thinking about her.

**Catherine**    No. Me neither.

**Marie Louise**    Twenty-eight weeks. Can you imagine it, Catherine? The poor, poor, poor, little. I hope you don't take this the wrong way, and I'm sure it must be complicated with, because I have a certain position and a certain amount of, well, money, but I think that you have, sometimes I think this, you have the capacity actually to exploit people and if I had to say one thing that I didn't like about you it would be that.

**Catherine**    Fucking hell.

**Marie Louise**    Don't swear.

**Catherine**    What?

**Marie Louise**    You swear all the time.

*Pause.*

Look!

**Catherine**    What?

**Marie Louise**    Out there!

**Catherine**    What?

**Marie Louise**    You can see the Wheel!

**Anne Schults**'s *house. Morning.* **Gary** *and* **Anne**. *She has stopped crying.*

**Anne**   What time is it?

**Gary**   It's eleven o'clock.

**Anne**   What am I going to do?

**Gary**   –

**Anne**   What am I going to do, Gary?

**Gary**   I –

**Anne**   Where's Robert?

**Gary**   At the station.

**Anne**   You need to go, don't you?

**Gary**   No.

**Anne**   What am I going to . . . ? I've got to go to Sainsbury's. I need to buy some food.

**Gary**   I could –

**Anne**   No. I want to. And I'll stop at the post office. There's something I should . . .

*She turns away suddenly, perhaps catches her breath.*

**Gary**   What?

**Anne**   I'm going to have to ring people. Or write to them.

**Gary**   Yes.

**Anne**   And talk to the, the, the radio people. All that.

**Gary**   We can help you with that.

**Anne**   I won't do an interview.

**Gary**   No.

**Anne**   We were going to go away! Me and John! Go to France! Can you imagine?

**Gary**    You could still . . .

**Anne**    But all of the things, we need to arrange things.
And invite people. There are people we want to to to see.
What am I going to do?

**Gary**    –

**Anne**    I'll have to sort out her bedroom. All her things.

**Gary**    If there's –

**Anne**    I'm going to go to the chemist. And I'm going to
clean the kitchen. And sort out all of the jars of food. Check
their sell-by dates. And clean the bathroom. I'm going to go
to his work. I'm going to find him and tell him.

*Blackout. One minute.*


**November**

*Gary addresses the audience.*

**Gary**    I'm heading down Charing Cross Road towards
Embankment. It's just starting to get dark. There are one or
two people just starting to finish work.

There are two children's toys, two toy bikes just parked,
parked by this tree by the side of the pub there . . . All the
plastic is blue and yellow, trashy. And I find it really
irritating that somebody has just left these things there. And
now with all these people, everybody just, just walking past
them. Like they don't give all that much.

I really want to get a drink.

There are these two homeless people on Embankment.
They're juggling. One of them is. Just juggling these two
poxy little batons, and his mate, who's younger than him,
has a hat with a little sign on and when I walk past them
they don't ask me or nothing but the way they look at me,
particularly that cunt with the sign, the young fucker, the

way he looks at me. Because I don't give them any money
or anything. Makes me want. How dare you make me feel
like that for what you're doing after all the things I've done
in my day.

I want to beat the shit out of them.

I can taste bitter and tobacco in my mouth.

I cross the bridge. Cross Hungerford Bridge. By this time it's
getting to be near enough five thirty. Stood over the water.
Looking through the metal slats at the river below. It's like,
for a second, it honestly sounds like the river has started to
roar. It looks, it just looks indomitable. And there's
something so truthful about that. That it has been there for
so long. And that it will survive me and survive all this. I feel
like it justifies me. That I am justified. Just because of the
size of the river. And the history. And it's getting cold but
that knowledge feels good. It feels important to know this.

And I get to the station.

I'm tired.

And I'm getting hungry.

And all I want to do is go home and go to bed with
someone.


*Outside* **Marie Louise***'s flat. Late afternoon.* **Catherine** *is
leaving. They wear coats.* **Marie Louise** *hugs her arms around
herself.* **Catherine** *has a bag at her feet.*

**Marie Louise**    Have you got everything?

**Catherine**    Yeah.

**Marie Louise**    If you've left anything I'll just –

**Catherine**    Sure.

**Marie Louise**    – give you a ring and you can . . . Or I
can send it to you.

**Catherine**   That would be –

**Catherine** *goes to pick up her bag.*

**Marie Louise**   I'm sorry.

**Catherine** (*stops*)   What for?

**Marie Louise**   For, y'know.

**Catherine**   Really. Don't be.

**Marie Louise**   I just get.

**Catherine** (*picks the bag up*)   I know.

**Marie Louise**   Sometimes.

**Catherine** (*swings it on to her shoulder*)   I'm exactly the same.

**Marie Louise**   Yeah. (*Looks up.*) The moon's out.

**Catherine** (*sees it*)   Early.

**Marie Louise**   I like that. This time of year.

**Catherine** (*turning to move away*)   Yeah.

**Marie Louise**   I'd love to go to the moon, me. One day. Look down on stuff.

**Catherine** (*looks at her for a while*)   I –

**Marie Louise**   Actually, you know what I'd love to do?

**Catherine**   What?

**Marie Louise**   I'd love to travel more. Spend some time. Take some time off. Go everywhere.

**Catherine**   Everywhere?

**Marie Louise**   All over the world.

**Catherine** (*smiling*)   You could probably afford that, couldn't you?

**Marie Louise**   What do you mean?

**Catherine**   Nothing, I just –

**Marie Louise**    What would you do?

**Catherine**    What?

**Marie Louise**    If you took time off? A whole, you know.

**Catherine**    I don't know.

**Marie Louise**    I'd love to read more. Just. Or study. I made such a mess of my, my, my . . . If I regretted anything I think it would be that.

**Catherine** *smiles. Looks away.*

**Catherine**    Yeah.

**Marie Louise**    How are you getting there?

**Catherine**    Go on the tube. Just a couple of stops.

**Marie Louise**    I could get you a taxi or something.

**Catherine**    No, it's nothing.

**Marie Louise**    And it's funny.

**Catherine**    What?

**Marie Louise**    Because I won't study. Or this whole, this writing thing. That won't happen. Or the singing.

*Pause.* **Catherine** *looks at her.*

**Marie Louise**    Do you know what I mean?

**Catherine**    Yeah.

**Marie Louise**    It won't, that won't. Which is a shame. I think. I wish you so much luck.

**Catherine**    Thank you.

**Marie Louise**    I so love the way you're, you get, you have this this passion.

**Catherine**    Thank you.

**Marie Louise**    And, in the future, if you had a child. Would you rather have a son or a daughter?

**Catherine**   A daughter, I think.

**Marie Louise**   I hope that you get a daughter then.

**Catherine**   One day.

**Marie Louise**   Yes. I know I must have let you down.

**Catherine**   –

**Marie Louise**   It's just . . . Do you know?

**Catherine**   What?

**Marie Louise**   I'd really, one day. I'd love to go back to Bloomsbury. Go back and live there. I'd love that. Just pack everything up into my boxes and my bags and just jolly well just go go go home.

**Catherine**   Would you?

**Marie Louise** (*looking away*)   I'd love that. I would just, just love it. I –

**Catherine**   You should calm down sometimes.

**Marie Louise**   What?

**Catherine**   Not get so nervous about things.

**Marie Louise**   No.

**Catherine**   Because. I think. You're very frank.

**Marie Louise**   Frank.

**Catherine**   And that's good.

**Marie Louise**   Thank you.

**Catherine**   Just . . .

**Marie Louise**   What?

**Catherine**   Nothing. Here.

*They go to hug but* **Catherine***'s bag makes it awkward, clumsy, shit.*

I'll see you soon, Marie Louise.

**Marie Louise**  You promise?


*Regent's Park. Morning. Within sight of the jackals' enclosure at London Zoo.* **Anne** *and* **Robert** *stand looking at them. They don't look at each other while they talk.*

*Beat. About the jackals.*

**Anne**  He looks bored.

**Robert**  Keeps scratching.

**Anne**  Are you cold?

**Robert**  No. No. I'm fine. Are you all right?

**Anne**  Yes. Thank you.

*Beat. She looks at him briefly then away again.*

Funny coming here. I've not been here for ages. It was good of you two to come all this way. There was something I – (*Smiling.*) I'm so odd sometimes. I'm sorry.

**Robert**  No. Really. Don't be sorry. God.

**Anne**  It's just the house is a bit of a mess. I was trying to think of somewhere and I remembered this place and I just thought. Silly.

**Robert**  I like it. I've never been here before.

*Pause.*

I like zoos. Looking at all the animals.

*Pause.*

The way they look at you. This way you don't even have to pay.

**Anne** (*smiles at him*)  How's Gary treating you?

**Robert**  All right. Yeah. Not bad.

**Anne** How's Gary treating himself?

**Robert** What do –

**Anne** He smokes too much. Drinks too much. It's stupid.

**Robert** He's. You know.

*Gary enters with three cups.*

**Gary** One tea (**Anne***'s*), one coffee white (**Robert***'s*) and one coffee black (*his own*).

*Some time. Looking at the enclosure.*

I like jackals.

*Some more.*

So. Brighton.

**Anne** Yeah.

**Gary** When?

**Anne** About three weeks.

**Gary** That'll be good. Yer know. Sea and that. Be beautiful.

**Anne** I hope so.

**Gary** No, I do. I think it's a really good idea.

**Anne** I just wanted to see you. To let you know.

**Gary** Yeah. That's good of you. Means a lot to us.

**Robert** Yeah.

**Anne** We got your flowers. They were lovely. Thank you.

**Gary** That's all right.

**Anne** She'd have been twelve. Funny. And then soon it's Christmas. And it won't be long now until it's a year. And that's another anniversary. Isn't it?

*They drink their drinks.*

I'm sure that one's looking at me.

*They smile.*

**Robert**   You gonna carry on teaching?

**Anne**   I think so. There's a post coming up, at the University of Sussex.

**Robert**   Oh yeah?

**Anne**   Yeah. But –

**Robert**   What?

**Anne**   Institutions. Sometimes, you know the song 'Rio' by Duran Duran?

**Robert**   Yeah.

**Anne**   When I was a kid that was my favourite song. I used to love Duran Duran. Sometimes. In the Senior Common Room. I just want to stand on a table and just sing it. Up at the top of my voice.

*Smiles. Some time.*

**Gary**   How's Mr Petrie?

**Anne**   He's all right. He had an affair.

**Gary**   –

**Anne**   Just a. Nothing serious. It's over now. We're doing all right. Eat a lot of fish and chips together. Watch a lot of television. He's still teaching. He's got a job in the, the media department. (*Pause.*) I used to think he was so beautiful. A little bit fat but – I used to love his eyes and the way he was so intelligent. Making a house for him.

**Gary**   Are you all right?

**Anne**   I'm fine. Yeah. Yes. Yes. I'm good.

**Gary**   We need to be going soon.

**Anne**   I used to come here with Billy Franks.

**Gary**   Who was Billy Franks?

**Anne**   Billy Franks was the first boy I ever kissed. When I was a girl. We used to come here at break times. I went to school just up in Camden. Come down to the zoo. I remember the first time I kissed him. How it felt. How soft his lips felt. Could be . . . And I split up with him. I ditched him. And made him cry. I'm telling him that I don't want to go out with him any more and he just starts crying. He's fourteen. Never saw him much after that. Never saw him at all after I left school. Wonder what he's doing now. I'd love to, just, to see him. Tell him I'm sorry.

*Pause. The three stare out. Drink their tea and coffee.*

**Anne**   Do you think we're getting old, Gary?

**Gary**   Yeah.

**Anne**   Does it bother you?

**Gary**   I don't think about it.

*Some time.*

**Anne**   There was – I wanted to – I bought a present for the two of you. But I left it at home. I decided not to. I'm going to post it to you. Is that all right?

**Gary**   Yeah. Of course.

**Robert**   What is it?

**Anne**   You'll find out.

*She turns to* **Gary***, holds his hand.*

**Anne**   I like the way you're, you seem, you seem quite sad to me. I quite like that. You should be going.

**Gary**   Yes.

**Anne**   Gary, if you find him, when, when you find him. I
don't ever want to see him. Because I know I could, I, I
could actually *kill* him.

*Pause.*

The idea that he breathes.

**Gary**   Yeah.


**Anne** *addresses the audience.*

**Anne**   I'm. I'm trying to . . . remember. I'm trying to
remember how to walk. Trying to understand how to walk.
I'm heading south from the university through Gordon
Square and I'm thinking very, very hard about how you put
one foot in front of, in front of the other and do you ever,
when you, lift both feet?

I am avoiding eye contact.

I have it in my head that the safest thing would be to avoid
standing on, on any cracks or gaps in the pavement.

They've started to put up Christmas lights in the trees.

I can smell fire but nobody else seems to notice or be
worried so it might just be me.

There's a dry rain on my hair, it's so light that I don't
actually even notice it getting wet.

Just on the south-east corner of the square there's a man in
a completely white suit. He's very drunk. He's maybe fifty
years old. And he's yelling at the sky. He's really furious,
really ferocious.

One woman, working in one of the cafes there, she has this
smile this big, big, big, big smile. It's lovely.

And all these people are all still cleaning windows. And
driving buses. And working in their, in their, their shops.
They're all still doing all of that.

I panic about stopping. I decide that I mustn't stop. I mustn't stop. Because I don't know what would happen to me if I stopped. How I would be able to start again.

And I'm getting to the tube station at Russell Square. Right there. Just right in front of it by the fruit stand and the flower stand and the newspaper vendor. By the cinema. With all the people. And the sun comes out.

**Gary** *and* **Robert** *in a parked car outside a house in Hackney. Lunchtime. The two are completely transfixed by the house they are staking.*

**Robert**   You think it was him?

*Pause.*

You think he'll come back?

**Gary**   I don't know.

*Silence.*

**Robert**   Can I tell you something?

**Gary**   Go on.

**Robert**   I was going to put in for a request to transfer. Back up north. Or to another force. I didn't think I could – I got as far as arranging a meeting with the CI. Part of the reason was because you were doing my fucking head in so much.

**Gary**   I see.

**Robert**   I didn't.

**Gary**   No.

**Robert**   I decided not to.

**Gary**   Good.

**Robert**   You think we'll get him?

**Gary**   I don't have a clue.

*Some time.*

**Robert**   I finished with Esther.

**Gary**   You what?

**Robert**   Last night. Finished it.

**Gary**   How come?

**Robert**   It was just. It was getting just too. All the gabbing on about a baby and that. We were just at each other's throats. Yer with me? It was mental.

**Gary**   Right.

**Robert**   She cried. Quite badly actually. Did my head in a bit.

**Gary**   But you didn't let her back.

**Robert**   No. No. No. I didn't. But fucking drives yer mental, doesn't it?

**Gary**   Yes. It does.

**Robert**   Can I ask you something?

**Gary**   What?

**Robert**   How long have you known Jenny?

**Gary**   Since school.

**Robert**   Long time.

**Gary**   Not always going out with her all that time.

**Robert**   No?

**Gary**   No.

**Robert**   What is it?

**Gary**   What?

**Robert**   That makes you just know?

**Gary**   What do you mean?

**Robert**   What did you like about her?

**Gary**   Lots of things.

**Robert**   What like?

**Gary**   I always admired the way she did everything properly.

**Robert**   You what?

**Gary**   And then, when she got to about seventeen, almost overnight almost I just thought, 'My God! You are just gorgeous.'

**Robert**   And you still do?

**Gary**   I think so.

**Robert**   Do you love her?

**Gary**   Course.

**Robert**   What do you love about her?

**Gary**   She's very honest. She doesn't put up with any nonsense. Doesn't let me go on. I trust her. (*Beat.*) Sometimes I could just leave her.

**Robert**   Really?

**Gary**   Sometimes I think I've let her down quite badly.

**Robert**   How?

**Gary**   Just . . .

**Robert**   What?

**Gary**   You know what I want to do?

**Robert**   What?

**Gary**   I want to find the cunts who saw Daisy go and did nothing and just, just, just –

**Robert**   What?

**Gary**    Tell them. Ask them what they did. Sometimes I think . . .

**Robert**    What, Gary?

**Gary**    I'm not as good at this job as I once was, Robert, you with me?

*Long pause.*

**Robert**    You know what I think?

**Gary**    What?

**Robert**    What I really think about you?

**Gary**    What?

**Robert**    I like the way you can be very honest sometimes. And I think that you are a good copper. Still. But you're a moody fucker. You need to just relax a bit. Tell a few jokes. Stop drinking so much fucking booze and coffee. 'Cause you'll just die. And stop treating me like I'm a prick. 'Cause I'm not. Or thinking you can stop all bad things or know people better than they know themselves because you fucking just can't. And I think that you're never going to get away. Go to the Isle of Man. Any of that. It isn't going to happen. That's a bit –

**Gary**    What?

**Robert**    I don't know.

**Gary**    You're quite angry sometimes, aren't you? I quite like that.

**Gary** *punches* **Robert**'s *arm affectionately but not gently. Turns away.*

**Robert**    I like you.

**Gary**    You what?

**Robert**    I was going to thank you for not grassing on me when I freaked out on you.

**Gary**   You didn't. Not really.

**Robert**   You're all right. You know? You are. You . . .

**Gary**   What?

**Robert**   Just –

*Very, very long pause.*

# Country Music

This play is dedicated
to those teachers and writers I worked with
in HMP Wandsworth and HMP Grendon and
YOT Salford and YOT Kensington and Chelsea
between 2001 and 2003.

*Country Music* was first performed at the Royal Court Jerwood Theatre Upstairs, London, on 24 June 2004. The cast was as follows:

| | |
|---|---|
| **Jamie Carris** | Lee Ross |
| **Lynsey Sergeant** | Sally Hawkins |
| **Matty Carris** | Calum Callaghan |
| **Emma Carris** | Laura Elphinstone |

| | |
|---|---|
| *Director* | Gordon Anderson |
| *Designer* | Soutra Gilmour |
| *Lighting* | Charles Balfour |
| *Composer* | Julian Swales |

## Characters

**Jamie Carris**, *eighteen/twenty-nine/thirty-nine*
**Lynsey Sergeant**, *fifteen*
**Matty Carris**, *nineteen*
**Emma Carris**, *seventeen*

## Setting

The play takes place in Thurrock, Essex; Her Majesty's
Prison Grendon, Buckinghamshire; and Durham Road,
Sunderland, between 1983 and 2004.

A dash ( – ) denotes interruption or a sudden halt
An ellipsis ( . . . ) denotes a trailing off

## One

*Friday 15 July 1983, 2 a.m.*

*A parked Ford Cortina in the car park of a service garage on the A13 east of Thurrock.*

**Jamie Carris**, *eighteen years old, sits in the driver's seat. He is drinking coffee from a paper cup.*

**Lynsey Sergeant**, *fifteen years old, sits in the passenger seat.*

**Jamie**   You reckon they will?

**Lynsey**   Yeah.

**Jamie**   Check the beds?

**Lynsey**   Always do now. New night warden. Does bed checks. Window checks. Everything.

**Jamie**   Reckon they'll suss yer?

**Lynsey**   Course.

*He starts chuckling. She joins in after a while.*

**Jamie**   What'll they do?

**Lynsey**   I don't know. Go mad prob'ly. Crack up. Have a fucking eppy. Call the Old Bill.

**Jamie**   Will they?

**Lynsey**   I dunno. Sometimes do. Sometimes can't be arsed.

*She sits forward in the passenger seat. Staring hard out of the front window.*

**Jamie** *turns to look at her.*

**Jamie**   You cold?

**Lynsey**   No.

**Jamie**   You want my jumper?

**Lynsey**   I'm all right.

**Jamie**   You're funny.

**Lynsey**   Why?

**Jamie**   Look at yer.

**Lynsey**   What about me?

**Jamie** (*smiles*)   Nothing. (*Drinks. Holds cup in his teeth. Grins at her.*) You hungry?

**Lynsey**   No, I'm all right.

**Jamie**   You want a packet of crisps? I've got fucking hundreds.

*He reaches behind his seat to the back seat and pulls out a squashed multi-pack of crisps. Starts to rifle through the different packets.*

**Lynsey** (*laughs at the amount of crisps*)   No, thank you. Honestly. I'm all right.

**Jamie**   All fucking flavours and all. Salt and vinegar. Cheese and onion. Beef. Here. Have one.

**Lynsey**   Bad for yer, them. Rot yer teeth.

**Jamie**   Fuck off.

**Lynsey**   Make yer fat.

**Jamie**   No they won't. Have one.

**Lynsey**   No.

*She sticks her tongue out at him.*

**Jamie**   Starve to death, you. I'm meant to look after you. You'll waste away. (*Beat.*) Anyway. (*Grins at her.*) I like a bit of fat, me.

**Lynsey**   Jamie.

**Jamie**   I do. Bit of a tummy.

*He opens his packet. Takes a mouthful.*

**Lynsey**    You think I'm fat?

**Jamie**    No. Just saying. Should have one.

*Pause.*

I like prawn cocktail best.

**Lynsey** (*imitating*) 'I like prawn cocktail best.'

*He laughs at her. Bounces himself as far forward as her in his seat.*

**Jamie**    That was fucking great. Weren't it, Lynse? Weren't that fucking smart?

**Lynsey** *starts to chuckle slightly.*

**Lynsey**    Yeah.

**Jamie** (*acting out his driving with his right hand*)    Fucking handbreak turns. Bouff. Nnnyyyeeeoowwww. Give it! Fucking tell yer.

**Lynsey** *laughs at him.*

**Jamie**    Mad fucking Max, mate. Fucking Rambo.

**Lynsey**    Dickhead.

**Jamie**    You wait till they finish the motorway, Lynse. Gonna build a big old bridge, and everything. See us then, tell yer, I'll be fucking dynamite. (*Beat.*) You done the old tunnel before?

**Lynsey**    The what?

**Jamie**    Going south, out of Thurrock, you ever done that?

**Lynsey**    No.

**Jamie**    Should do. It's quality. I do it. Bomb it. Fucking overtaking and everything.

**Lynsey**    You're full of shit, you.

**Jamie**    Am not.

**Lynsey**    Yer've never done that.

**Jamie**   Yes I have.

**Lynsey**   How come yer never took us then?

**Jamie**   Never wanted to. Yer whinge too much.

**Lynsey**   Shut it, you.

**Jamie** *laughs. Sits back down. Puts his feet up on the steering wheel.*

**Jamie**   You comfy?

**Lynsey**   Yeah.

**Jamie**   You sure?

**Lynsey**   Yeah.

**Jamie**   Put your seat back.

**Lynsey**   I said I'm all right, didn't I?

**Jamie**   You gonna go to sleep?

**Lynsey**   Might do in a bit. I'm all right for now.

**Jamie**   Should do. Just go to sleep whenever you want. I don't mind driving with people asleep. Some people can't do it. Doesn't bother me. I only need a little bit of a break. Won't be long. Have a quick break and we'll crack on.

*He pulls a bottle of tequila from under his seat and necks a mouthful.*

You want some of this, Lynsey?

**Lynsey**   No, thanks. I'm all right.

**Jamie** *(coughs, half giggles)*   Should have some. Fucking does the business. Telling yer.

**Lynsey**   You reckon?

**Jamie**   Hits the fucking, the spot, the. Tell yer. Hits it. Bang. Like that.

**Lynsey**   Shouldn't drink and drive.

**Jamie**   Fuck off.

**Lynsey**   Should yer, though?

**Jamie**   I'm all right. I'm better, me, with a bit of a drink. I see stuff clearer.

**Lynsey**   Psycho.

**Jamie**   Bit of coffee and that. Bit of Coke. I'm away.

**Lynsey** *watches as he slugs another tequila. Puts the bottle back and pulls a can of Coke from under the same seat. Opens it.*

**Jamie**   When we get there. I'm going doing the laundrettes, Lynsey. You coming?

**Lynsey**   The laundrettes?

**Jamie**   Go down Poynter's Lane. Sutton Road. Get some cash.

**Lynsey**   How?

**Jamie**   Just smash up the coin slots. Get a crowbar. It's easy. Nobody says anything.

**Lynsey**   Could do.

**Jamie**   Get some chips, couldn't we, for our tea?

**Lynsey**   Where we staying?

**Jamie**   I'm gonna get us a hotel.

**Lynsey**   Are yer?

**Jamie**   Get one on the seafront. Be fucking smart.

**Lynsey**   I've never been Southend before.

**Jamie**   Ain't yer?

**Lynsey**   No.

**Jamie**   It's quality. Swear. Better than fucking Margate.

**Lynsey**   You got some money for a hotel, Jamie?

**Jamie**   Course. It'll be sound.

*Offers her the can.*

You want some Coke?

**Lynsey**    No, thank you. I'm all right.

**Jamie** *finishes his drink. Starts chuckling.*

**Jamie**    Guess who I'm thinking about?

**Lynsey**    Who?

**Jamie**    No, go on, have a guess.

**Lynsey**    Fuck off, Jamie, who?

**Jamie**    Mr Mackenzie.

**Lynsey** (*laughing*)    You should have seen him.

**Jamie**    I can imagine. Mad bird, you.

*Slight pause.*

It's funny. If he saw us, I wonder what he'd think.

**Lynsey**    I don't know.

**Jamie**    Probably think. Probably think. Probably think, yeah. That's fucking typical. I am not surprised one fucking second. Don't yer reckon?

**Lynsey**    Probably get dead jealous. Wish he was doing it too.

**Jamie** *smiles at her.*

*A slight pause.*

**Lynsey**    Don't spend too much money. On the hotel. Will yer?

**Jamie**    No. Don't panic. Just get a nice one. Nice B & B or summit.

**Lynsey**    You gonna get a job, Jamie?

**Jamie**    Course.

**Lynsey**   What job you gonna get, you think?

**Jamie**   Fucking, a good one.

**Lynsey**   Could we get a flat, you reckon? After a bit?

**Jamie**   Yeah. Or a house. If we move out a little bit. Get a little house.

**Lynsey**   Get a garden.

**Jamie**   Could do. Be good, wouldn't it?

**Lynsey**   Be fucking great.

*A slight pause.*

**Lynsey**   What time is it now?

**Jamie**   Quarter past two.

**Lynsey**   Funny. I'm not tired at all.

**Jamie**   You should try and sleep, though. You'll feel better for it.

*Beat.*

**Lynsey**   Where did you get the car?

**Jamie**   Up Valley Parade.

**Lynsey**   It's good, i'n't it?

**Jamie**   I think it's great.

**Lynsey**   I like the headrests. They're well comfy.

*She leans her head back on hers to test it.*

**Jamie**   I was gonna ask you something.

**Lynsey**   What?

**Jamie**   In a bit. Not for a while. Not for years maybe. You think Matty could come stay with us?

**Lynsey**   Yeah.

**Jamie**   Be good, wouldn't it, if he did? When he's older and that.

**Lynsey**   Be great. I like Matty.

**Jamie**   Can be a bit of a little dick at times but he's not too bad normally.

**Lynsey**   He's only eight.

**Jamie**   Yeah.

**Lynsey**   He's eight, you're eighteen, Jamie. Course you think he's a dick. (*Beat.*) I think he's quite sweet.

**Jamie**   Be like having a kid.

**Lynsey**   Fuck off.

**Jamie** (*smirks*)   I might get another coffee.

**Lynsey**   All right.

**Jamie**   Then I think we should maybe fuck off.

**Lynsey**   Right.

**Jamie**   Should only take an hour. Max. If we put a bit of speed on.

**Lynsey**   Right. Good. Jamie . . .

**Jamie**   Yeah?

**Lynsey**   You reckon your mum'll notice you've gone?

**Jamie**   I dunno. Maybe. (*He chuckles.*) Fucking psycho. Sick of her.

**Lynsey**   You reckon they'll be looking for yer?

**Jamie**   Who?

**Lynsey**   Filth.

**Jamie**   I don't know.

**Lynsey**   Be looking for the car, though, won't they?

**Jamie**   I don't know. I don't reckon they bother any more. About cars and that.

**Lynsey**   I think they will.

**Jamie**   They'll start looking south, though. Bet yer. They'll go down Margate. Won't think about crossing the river. Will they? Won't think about that. They're not smart.

**Lynsey**   Did you kill him?

**Jamie** (*splutters a laugh*)   Did I what?

**Lynsey**   Gary Noolan. Did you kill him, do yer think?

**Jamie** (*still laughing*)   Oh for fuck's sake, Lynsey.

**Lynsey**   Did yer, Jamie?

**Jamie** (*still*)   Course I didn't kill him. Fucking. I only. 'Did you kill him.' Yer monghead.

**Lynsey**   Well, I don't know, do I? Might have done. Do my head in if you did.

**Jamie**   Well, I didn't. So just.

**Lynsey**   You reckon you're gonna get sent down?

**Jamie**   You what?

**Lynsey**   Last time they said you might go Borstal. Go East Sussex.

**Jamie** *laughs at her.*

**Lynsey**   I'm just worried about you.

**Jamie**   Well, just don't be.

**Lynsey**   Jamie. I don't even know what you did. Not properly. You just turn up. Beep your fucking horn. 'Get in. We're fucking off.' I'm like, 'All right, Jamie. Nice car.'

**Jamie**   I told you.

**Lynsey**   No you never.

**Jamie**   I went down Stationers. Looking for Gary Noolan. After he'd left ours. After he'd left our mum's. After I saw you. And I found him. And I glassed the cunt. I went down the offie. Wanted some fags. And a bottle of tequila. And some crisps. Didn't have any money. This kid started getting lippy. So I stabbed him. Took all the stuff. Went outside. (*About the car.*) Found this cunt down Valley Parade. Came and found you. I thought you'd be happy.

**Lynsey**   You never told me about the kid.

**Jamie**   You what?

**Lynsey**   You never did.

**Jamie**   It's not a big deal.

**Lynsey**   How old was he?

**Jamie**   Fucksake.

**Lynsey**   How old was he, Jamie?

**Jamie**   What does it matter?

**Lynsey**   Matters to me.

**Jamie**   I don't know. I don't know how old he was. Sixteen.

**Lynsey**   Right.

**Jamie** *pulls the tequila out again and slugs some. Wipes his mouth. Stares at her. Smiles at her.*

**Jamie**   Do you want a bit of this?

*Offers the tequila.*

**Lynsey**   Yeah.

*Takes the tequila. Wipes the neck. Drinks.*

**Jamie**   Do you want some crisps?

*Offers the multi-pack again.*

**Lynsey**   Yeah.

**Jamie**  Got cheese and onion. Salt and vinegar. Beef.
Roast chicken. Ready salted.

**Lynsey**  Salt and vinegar.

**Jamie**  Here.

**Lynsey**  Thanks.

**Lynsey** *takes a packet of crisps and opens it. They eat. Short time.*

**Lynsey**  I reckon they will find you.

*A slight pause.*

I just thought I'd say that.

*A slight pause.* **Jamie** *sits forward again, eyes lit up.*

**Jamie** *sniggers.*

**Jamie**  Should we do a house?

**Lynsey**  What?

**Jamie**  Us two. Go and do a house. When we get up
Southend. Find a big one, one of the big houses there. Up
seafront. Wakering Road. You should see them. They've got
fucking everything.

**Lynsey**  Stop it.

**Jamie**  Hi-fis. Videos. Posh carpets. The works. We'd
make a packet. Do a piss. Do a shit on the floor. I'm gonna
do that, I reckon.

**Lynsey**  Stop it, Jamie.

**Jamie**  Stop what?

**Lynsey**  You know.

**Jamie**  No. Stop what? Stop what, Lynsey? Stop what?
Come on. Fucking hell!

*He thumps the dashboard.*

*Pause.*

**Lynsey** *clocks him before she speaks.*

**Lynsey**   What'd happen to Matty?

**Jamie**   You what?

**Lynsey**   If you got sent down. What'd happen to Matty? Who'd look after him? Your mum?

**Jamie**   He'd be all right.

**Lynsey**   Can I tell you something?

**Jamie**   I'd –

**Lynsey**   I think you're wrong about the cops.

**Jamie**   You what?

**Lynsey**   I think they'll be looking for you. I think they'll know to look for the car and I think they'll know that you've been the one who's nicked it. I don't think they're as thick as you think they are.

**Jamie**   Don't you?

**Lynsey**   If you went back, hand yerself, write a statement, a, a, a confession or something.

**Jamie**   Do what?

**Lynsey**   I think might make a difference.

**Jamie**   Fuck off.

**Lynsey**   To the way they treat you.

**Jamie**   Fuck off.

**Lynsey**   To your sentence or, or, or –

**Jamie**   Fuck off, Lynsey. Fuck off. Just fuck off, would you? Christ!

**Lynsey**   I'm right, aren't I?

**Jamie**   No.

**Lynsey**   I am. Course I am. You know I am.

**Jamie** –

**Lynsey** I want to go home.

**Jamie** Oh!

**Lynsey** I want to go back to the home.

**Jamie** You got to be kidding.

**Lynsey** I wanna go back to Clarence House, I'm worried about what they'll say.

**Jamie** Swear. Lynsey.

**Lynsey** It's all right for you, Jamie. I ain't got nowhere else to go.

**Jamie** Look at me.

**Lynsey** They've not been as bad to me as they were to you.

**Jamie** Do you know what would happen?

**Lynsey** I don't care.

**Jamie** You can't. You can't go. You can't go home. You can't.

**Lynsey** I'm going.

**Jamie** You want me to smack yer? Do yer? 'Cause I will. I fucking will.

**Lynsey** You what?

**Jamie** I'll smack yer face.

**Lynsey** Don't you talk to me like that.

**Jamie** I fucking don't believe you, Lynsey, Christ.

**Lynsey** Think you're so hard.

**Jamie** Don't you push it.

**Lynsey** You fucking do, though. Think yer the big man. Yer fucking not. Yer fucking just –

**Jamie** *hits her head with the ball of his open palm.*

**Lynsey**   Ow. That hurt me.

**Jamie** *does it again. Makes her hit her head against the side of the car.*

**Lynsey**   Get off.

**Jamie**   Fuck you.

*He does it again. She starts crying.*

Stop crying. Stop crying. Stop fucking crying. What they gonna say now? Eh? Fucking cunts. Clarence House. Fucking. You should see your face.

**Lynsey** *tries the door.*

**Jamie**   It's locked. Don't try it 'cause it's fucking locked.

*Long pause.*

**Lynsey** *wipes her eyes.*

**Lynsey**   Take me home, please.

**Jamie**   Fuck off.

**Lynsey**   Please, Jamie.

**Jamie**   Fuck off.

**Lynsey**   I'll get back anyway. Go on the fucking train. I'll tell 'em you hit us if you don't. Tell 'em all. Tell Ross Mack.

**Jamie** (*beat first*)   You wouldn't.

**Lynsey**   Things he did to you, Jamie. He'd do 'em again if I asked him to. Mad boy, that one. Do anything I tell him.

**Jamie**   You fucking wouldn't.

**Lynsey**   You could always hang yerself again, Jamie, eh? (*Beat.*) I wouldn't lift yer down next time.

*She looks at him.*

*Slight pause.*

**Jamie** *looks out of the side window.*

**Lynsey**   Fucking hotel. Are you mental or what? How would you, couldn't even sign in. Could yer? Thick cunt. Big spastic.

*Slight pause.*

**Jamie** *bites his bottom lip.*

**Jamie**   Go to sleep.

**Lynsey**   You're joking, aren't yer?

**Jamie**   .Ruined it now.

**Lynsey**   Please let me out of the car.

**Jamie**   You not talking to us now? Is that it?

**Lynsey**   I hate you now.

**Jamie**   I don't know what you hate me for 'cause this is all your fault.

**Lynsey**   You what?

**Jamie**   Could have come up earlier on. Could have come this afternoon. Straight after I saw 'em. Straight after you came out. If you didn't want to go back Clarence House.

*Pause.*

I even asked yer. Didn't I? Didn't I, though?

*Long pause.* **Lynsey** *turns away from him.*

**Jamie** *drinks some more Coke.*

*Lights another cigarette. Smokes it.*

**Jamie**   Ross Mack's a fucking pussy.

*Finishes his cigarette. Takes as long as it takes him to smoke it.*

*Winds down his window and throws it out.*

Please stay with us.

*Slight pause.*

I'm sorry I hit you.

*Slight pause.*

I'm sorry I hit you, Lynsey, please stay with us.

*Slight pause.*

It never hurt yer, did it?

*He goes to stroke her.* **Lynsey** *winces away at first, but then lets him stroke her hair.*

**Lynsey**   Course it fucking hurt me, you thick bastard.

**Jamie**   I reckon we could get away, y'know? I reckon we could. Dump this car. Get another. Fuck right off. We could go up Scotland or something. The two of us. You looking after us. Me doing driving and that. Couldn't we, Lynsey? Don't yer reckon?

**Lynsey**   No.

**Jamie**   Why not? Why not, though?

**Lynsey**   I wouldn't want to. We couldn't anyway.

**Jamie**   We could, though, Lynsey, couldn't we? I reckon we could. I reckon it'd be fucking easy, Lynse. Be a piece of piss, mate. It'd be all right.

**Lynsey**   Jamie –

**Jamie**   Fucking hell!

**Lynsey**   You're not thinking.

**Jamie**   I am so thinking. I am thinking like, like, like, like. Please.

**Lynsey**   No.

**Jamie**   Yer gonna make me do it on my own, Lynsey? 'Cause I will.

**Lynsey**    Should have thought about that. Shouldn't yer? Shouldn't you?

**Jamie** *looks away from her. Gathers his breath. Holds his head up to the roof of the car. Squeezes his eyes closed tight. Looks back to her. Some time.*

**Lynsey**    You should go home. All the cops. I think it'd be all right, if you go home.

**Jamie**    Do yer?

**Lynsey**    I think it might be.

**Jamie** *grins. Swigs from the tequila.*

**Jamie**    Yer ever get like yer wanna cut yer eyes out?

*He wipes his mouth with the back of his hand.*

I remember when I was a kid.

*The two stare out, unable to look at one another.*

*The lights fall.*


**Two**

*Tuesday 13 September 1994, 2.15 p.m. The visiting room of Her Majesty's Prison Grendon, Buckinghamshire.*

*A white table with a blue Formica top. Two blue plastic chairs.*

*There is a constant noise of echoes. Steel. Shouts. Incoherent. Ever present.*

**Matty Carris**, *nineteen years old, stands above one of the chairs. He has a jacket on over a jumper and black jeans.* **Jamie Carris** *stands across the room from him.* **Jamie** *is wearing a grey sweatshirt, grey sweatpants and trainers. He is thicker-set than we last saw him. Tougher. More muscular. He is twenty-nine years old. He is in the fifth year of what will be a fourteen-year stretch.*

*The two stare at each other for a short while.*

**Jamie**　You have to sit down.

**Matty**　What?

**Jamie**　You can't stand up. They have to do checks on you if you touch us. You have to sit down. I'm sorry.

**Matty**　Right.

*Very long pause. The two men examine each other's face and then, led by* **Jamie***, they break into smiles.*

**Jamie**　Hello, Matty.

**Matty**　Hello, Jamie.

**Jamie**　How are you, mate?

**Matty**　I'm, I'm, I'm.

**Jamie**　It's good you're here.

**Matty**　Yeah. I. It's good to see you.

*Very long pause. The two of them stare at each other.*

It's funny as it goes.

**Jamie**　What is?

**Matty**　When I come in. They did a, one of them things, a rub-down on us.

**Jamie**　Oh yeah?

**Matty**　I got the, the giggles, didn't I? I couldn't help myself. It was ticklish.

**Jamie**　You fucking Muppet.

**Matty**　And the more I tried not to. The more I wanted to laugh. Fucking.

**Jamie**　What you like?

**Matty**　I know.

**Jamie**　You should sit down, mate.

**Matty**   Right.

*He does.* **Jamie** *sits with him.*

**Jamie**   Don't panic.

**Matty**   No. I won't. I'm all right.

*Pause. Then he nods, smiling encouragement.*

It's all right here. Innit?

**Jamie**   What?

**Matty**   I, when I was coming up. All the, the garden out front. That house and everything.

**Jamie**   Yeah.

**Matty**   I thought. Y'know? Looked all right.

**Jamie**   Yeah.

**Matty**   You get to do that, do yer?

**Jamie**   The garden?

**Matty**   Yeah.

**Jamie**   Not that one. No. Others.

**Matty**   Right. That's all right, innit?

**Jamie**   Yeah. Yeah. It's not bad. It's. That's another nick actually.

**Matty**   What?

**Jamie**   It is. There're two. This one. Springhill. Is the other one.

**Matty**   Bloody hell.

**Jamie**   Yeah.

**Matty**   Some places there are no prisons, are there? Here you can't fucking move for them.

**Jamie**   That's right.

**Matty**   Yeah.

**Jamie**   How was your journey?

**Matty**   Yeah. It was, easy. Y'know?

**Jamie**   Yeah?

**Matty**   Nice. Coming up through the country and that. Funny, innit?

**Jamie**   What?

**Matty**   The way this place just sits here. Don't notice it. Do yer? Until you're right here.

**Jamie**   No.

**Matty**   Takes yer by surprise, kind of, don't it?

**Jamie** *smiles. Tries to hold his eye contact.* **Matty** *can't.*

**Jamie**   Five year.

**Matty**   Yeah.

**Jamie**   Five years, Matty.

**Matty**   Yeah.

**Jamie**   You were thirteen.

**Matty**   Yeah.

**Jamie**   You want a cup of tea, mate?

**Matty**   What?

**Jamie**   You can get them. You ask them. They'll give you. I could murder a cup. They're like twenty pence or summink.

**Matty**   I can go.

**Jamie**   You got any money?

**Matty**   Yeah. Yeah. Yeah. Yeah.

**Jamie**    I can make us a, make us a rollie. You want a rollie?

**Matty**    Yeah. Go on.

**Jamie**    You go and get the teas and I'll.

**Matty**    Sure.

*Leaves* **Jamie** *rolling a cigarette. Hands shaking. Makes two. With real care. It's difficult for him to do this.*

*After a minute or so* **Matty** *returns with two cups of tea in polystyrene cups.*

**Matty**    Here you are.

**Jamie**    Beauty.

*Beat.* **Jamie** *stares at* **Matty**.

**Matty**    I bought you some tobacco. As it goes. Left it on the, on the, the, the, with the gate. They said it'd be all right.

**Jamie**    Yeah. They'll drop it over. Thank you.

**Matty**    And some phonecards I got yer.

**Jamie**    Right.

**Matty**    But you can't use them. Or summink. Is that right? You need special ones?

**Jamie**    Yeah.

**Matty**    I'll, next time.

**Jamie**    Yeah.

*He smiles. Beat.*

It was good to get your letter.

**Matty**    Yeah. I should have written sooner.

**Jamie**    I wish you had.

**Matty**    I know.

**Jamie**   I'm not angry or nothing. You were a fucking kid, eh? Can't blame yer for that. I just wish. Yer with me?

**Matty**   Yeah.

**Matty** *looks away from him. Tries to smile down into his teacup.*

**Jamie**   How's Mum?

**Matty**   She's OK. She's well. She's all right. Yeah. She told me to tell you. She's gonna try and come in. You send her a VO, she'll come in, definitely. She said.

**Jamie**   Right. Good. She doesn't need to.

**Matty**   No. She said she wanted to.

**Jamie**   Right. That's good. How's Al?

**Matty**   He's all right. Same really. Tell you what.

**Jamie**   What?

**Matty**   That, that, that queue. Fucking hell.

**Jamie**   What?

**Matty**   Some of them people in the, the, the waiting to come in.

**Jamie**   Yeah?

**Matty**   Fuck me. Fucking psychos. Fucking freaks. Worse out there than they are in here, half of them, I reckon.

**Jamie** *laughs, slurps his tea. Flicks ash.*

**Jamie**   Calm down.

**Matty**   What?

**Jamie**   You. Calm down. It's all right.

**Matty**   I am calm.

*Beat.*

**Jamie**   Good.

*Pause.*

**Matty**   It's funny. Standing at the gate. Thinking about all this. Back here. This building, when you're standing outside of it. Looking in. Waiting to come in. Bit fucking . . .

*Pause.*

I remember when you got out of East Sussex. After you glassed Gary Noolan.

**Jamie**   Oh yeah?

**Matty**   Coming up to meet yer. That was the same.

*Pause.*

**Jamie** *drinks his tea. Smiles.*

**Matty**   Is it different here?

**Jamie**   What?

**Matty**   To young offenders?

**Jamie** *(mouthful of tea)*   This place is a bit weird. All the therapy groups.

**Matty**   Right.

**Jamie** *goes into the pockets of his sweatpants.*

**Jamie**   You want a sweet?

**Matty**   What?

**Jamie**   I got some sweets, you want one?

**Matty**   Yeah. Go on then. Ta.

**Jamie** *passes him a sweet, which he puts in his mouth. The two of them chew for a while.*

**Jamie**   Can I call you Matt? Not Matty? Is that all right?

**Matty**   Yeah. Course you can. If you want to. Course.

**Jamie**   Sounds better. Don't it?

**Matty**   I don't know. Matt. Yeah. Sounds all right. I don't mind.

**Jamie**   Sounds better. (*Beat.*) Look at you.

**Matty**   What?

**Jamie**   Fucking shoulders on you!

**Matty**   What?

**Jamie**   You're like.

**Matty**   What?

**Jamie** *smiles. Doesn't answer. Relights his cigarette.*

**Jamie**   I might be getting day release.

**Matty**   You what?

**Jamie**   I might. They said. I'm up for my board next month. There's a possibility.

**Matty**   Fucking hell.

**Jamie**   I know.

**Matty**   That's . . .

**Jamie**   Come out. Go up London.

**Matty**   I'd come up and meet you.

**Jamie**   Be good.

**Matty**   Yeah.

**Jamie**   Just to see everybody. Go home.

**Matty**   Yeah. (*Beat.*) You wanna see the Bridge.

**Jamie**   They finished it, have they?

**Matty**   Couple of years back. You'd like it, I reckon.

*Beat.*

**Jamie**   How's, how's, how's college? How's college? Everything all right, yeah?

**Matty**    Yeah. Not bad. You know.

**Jamie**    What year you in now?

**Matty**    'S my second year.

**Jamie**    Second year. Right. And it's going all right, is it?

**Matty**    It's going. Yeah. I. It's going fine. Actually. Yeah.

*Pause.*

I was thinking of jacking it in a while back, as it goes.

**Jamie**    What?

**Matty**    I was thinking of knocking it on the head. College.

**Jamie**    Why?

**Matty**    I don't know really, just –

**Jamie**    What you wanna do that for? Don't be stupid. As if you wanna go round doing that.

**Matty**    I got a mate who's, he runs his own company. Does a bit of painting and decorating. Does houses. And bits of, y'know, chippying and that. Bit of bricklaying. He reckoned he could get us steady work. Take us on. Everything. I thought I might go and work with him. (*Beat.*) I might not. I've not decided.

**Jamie** *looks at him for a while. Sucks air between his teeth. Looks away, round the room at the other visits.*

**Matty**    What?

**Jamie** *looks back.*

**Jamie**    You seen Lynsey much?

**Matty**    Yeah. Bits.

**Jamie**    Seen Emma?

**Matty**    Yeah.

**Jamie**    How they doing?

**Matty**    I think they're all right.

**Jamie**    Are they?

**Matty**    Yeah.

**Jamie**    They ain't been in.

**Matty**    No?

**Jamie**    Four years.

**Matty**    Right.

**Jamie** *starts chewing on the nail of his right thumb as he talks.*

**Jamie**    It was my idea for them not to. It's not a good thing for a girl who's four. Y'know? She's four years old and they're asking her to take her fucking socks off and having a clock of them.

**Matty**    Right.

**Jamie**    So . . . . But they're all right?

**Matty**    I think they are, Jamie. Yeah.

**Jamie**    I should stop biting my nails.

**Matty**    Yeah.

**Jamie**    Fuckin' disgusting habit, I think.

*Smiles.*

*Pause.*

**Matty**    Jamie, Lynsey's moved up north.

*Pause.*

She met a bloke.

*Pause.*

She met some bloke and she moved up north with him and she took Emma with her.

*Pause.*

Moved up Sunderland.

*Pause.*

She came to, came to, came to, to tell us. Came round to the house. She wouldn't tell me where she was going exactly but she promised she'd try and phone me. Let us know.

*Pause.*

It was a month ago.

*Pause.*

She wanted me to come and see you. To tell you. She isn't going to come and see you herself, she said. She doesn't want Emma to come and see you. She doesn't want that.

*Pause.*

I never met him. I don't know who he is or what he's like. Or what he does. Or anything.

*Pause.* **Jamie** *nods over and over.*

**Jamie**    Right. Right. Right. Right. Right.

**Matty**    I haven't been able to sleep. Thinking about how I was going to tell you.

**Jamie**    Right.

**Matty**    Jamie, I'm really sorry, mate.

*Very long pause. Two staring at each other.* **Matty** *finds it difficult.*

**Jamie**    They didn't leave an address?

**Matty**    No.

**Jamie**    Will you ring them, find out?

**Matty**    I can't.

**Jamie**    Ring them, Matt. Somebody must know their number.

**Matty**    Jamie, it's not as . . .

**Jamie**    Not as what? Not as what? Matt? Not as what?

**Matty** Jamie, don't.

**Jamie** Don't what? Matt? Come on.

**Matty** This is difficult for me.

**Jamie** What is?

**Matty** This.

**Jamie** What did you say to her?

**Matty** I didn't know what to say.

**Jamie** Didn't yer?

**Matty** *looks away.*

*Pause.*

**Jamie** Five years I done for you.

**Matty** Don't.

**Jamie** I haven't seen you. You never wrote to me.

**Matty** I couldn't.

**Jamie** I only did it 'cause of you, mate.

**Matty** Don't say that.

**Jamie** I come out of East Sussex and you're a fucking child.

**Matty** I didn't ask you to do nothing.

**Jamie** And you're swanning round Stone Street with fucking Ross Mack, like you're his little fucking prime piece of pussy! Matty, you have no idea –

**Matty** I could have sorted him out.

**Jamie** What he was like. What he could do. What he did to me. The things he did to us. He was a proper nonce, Matty. I come out and he's hanging around you like a, like a, like a –

**Matty** You didn't need to do what you did.

**Jamie**  And she's telling you *that* and you didn't know what to say to her? Fucking hell!

**Matty**  You can't blame me.

**Jamie**  Don't cry. Not in here.

**Matty**  I'm not crying! (*Beat.*) I wanted to tell you myself. I didn't want you to find out from anybody else.

**Jamie**  Didn't yer?

**Matty**  No.

**Jamie**  Well, that's fucking –

**Matty**  That was important to me.

*Pause.*

I think about you all the time.

*Pause.*

**Jamie**  Shake my hand.

*No response.*

Matt.

**Matty** *is reluctant.*

**Jamie**  Here. Matt. Shake my hand. Shake my hand, Matt.

*He does.* **Jamie** *holds* **Matty**'s *hand longer and tighter than* **Matty** *wants him to.*

**Jamie**  Is that the only reason you came?

**Matty**  No, course it's not.

**Jamie**  Is that the only reason you've come in to see me, Matt?

**Matty**  Jamie, no. It isn't.

**Jamie**  'Cause if it is.

**Matty**   It isn't, I swear.

*Pause.*

**Jamie**   You know how you sometimes you have to, with a woman, you have to spit in their face, don't you? Because you can't hit a woman, can you? So that's what you have to do. Isn't it, Matt?

**Matty**   I don't know.

*Longer pause.* **Jamie** *strokes* **Matty**'s *held hand with his free hand.*

**Jamie**   How's Mum really?

**Matty**   What?

**Jamie**   How's Mum really?

**Matty**   I don't know.

**Jamie**   They won't let us out. To see her. Isn't gonna happen.

**Matty**   No.

**Jamie**   Have you the ability to count to ten? Can you spell your name?

**Matty**   You what?

**Jamie**   Nothing. Don't matter.

*He still holds* **Matty**'s *hand. Long pause.*

**Jamie**   The first nick I was in was called HMP Risley. They send a lot of lifers there to start their sentence. One night. Two weeks in. I'm on the balcony. In the middle of the wing. I hear these shouts going out. 'GET BEHIND THE DOORS! BANG UP! BANG UP! NOW!' Whole landing's clear of cons in two minutes. When that happens you know something's gonna go. I look out. I'm trying to clock what's going down. There are seven or eight screws positioning themselves outside a cell on the landing below mine. There's this woman, woman officer, opens the flap on the door. And you can only just hear her talking inside. She

unlocks the door. Draws her whistle. Which you don't do.
'Cause they're for fucking, for, for, for emergency. And she
blows it. And they pile in. Seven or eight of them. And what
they do is they start beating the fuck out of this, what I find
out later, is a, a, a boy. The fucking screams from him. They
break his hand. Bash it against the door. He's screaming for,
for, for minutes. And the thing is. He keeps apologising.
Keeps promising over and over to be good. And she's giving
it 'Break his arm! Break his arm!'

*Long pause.*

This does for me, this.

**Matty**    What?

**Jamie**    Seeing you.

**Matty**    Why?

**Jamie** *doesn't answer. He lets go of* **Matty***'s hand.*

*He takes out another sweet. Offers one to* **Matty***, who takes it.*
*Doesn't open it.* **Jamie** *opens his with real care. Looks at it before he*
*puts it in his mouth.*

**Matty**    I keep seeing Ross Mack's cousin. Keeps saying
what he's gonna do to yer. When you get out.

**Jamie**    Right.

**Matty**    Shouldn't have fucking done it. Should yer?
Should yer, though, Jamie? Really? Should yer?

**Jamie**    –

**Matty**    I never asked you to.

**Jamie**    No.

*Long pause.* **Matty** *rubs his eyes with the ball of his fist.*

**Jamie**    Will you try and find an address for me? Or a
phone number or something? Where they've gone. Will yer?
Will yer? Will yer, Matty? Please.

**Matty**    I'll try.

*Pause.*

**Jamie**    See this mark. On my finger. Fading now. See that? See my ring? Emma/Lynsey cut into it. Won't let us wear it now. I want a photograph of her. Of Emma. Lynsey won't send us one. I've asked her. Will you get us one?

**Matty**    I'll try.

**Jamie**    Will yer? A recent one.

**Matty**    Yeah.

*Long pause.*

**Jamie**    Would've been good, eh? To've watched her . . . y'know.

**Matty**    Shouldn't have hit Lynsey, then. Shouldn't hit people. Should yer? Should yer, though. Jamie?

**Jamie**    Don't, Matty.

Just.

Honest.

*He looks away from him.*

*Pause.*

I don't even dream about outside any more. Not for ages.

*Pause.*

**Matty**    If you get a day out, after that, when's your sentence review?

**Jamie** (*looks back*)    Two years, maybe.

**Matty**    What'll they say?

**Jamie**    Don't know. Early to tell. Maybe go to a day-release nick. Just banged up at weekends and night-time.

**Matty**    That'd be good. Wouldn't it? Wouldn't it, though?

**Jamie**    Yeah. I think so.

**Matty**    How long we got here?

**Jamie**    Five minutes. Max. Prob'ly less. Just finish it.
When they feel like it sometimes.

**Matty**    Right.

*Pause.*

I'm not coping, mate.

*Pause.*

I need you at home.

*Pause.*

Mum's started talking weird shit. All the time. She's. Dad's
no fucking use.

*Long pause.*

**Jamie**    If you come again will yer bring us some
magazines? Some baccy. Some fucking more tea bags.
That's good. Do that.

**Matty**    Yeah. Jamie. I'm sorry about Lynsey. About
Emma and that. I don't know what else to say about it.

**Jamie**    No.

**Matty**    I should fuck off.

**Jamie**    Wait.

**Matty**    Mad this, innit?

**Jamie**    When they call us. You're not allowed to stand up.
All right?

**Matty**    Right.

**Jamie**    Mum don't need to come. She's not well. Tell her,
tell her, tell her.

**Matty**    What?

**Jamie**    Nothing. Just make sure she's. You know.

*He leans over and touches **Matty**'s face. **Matty** is embarrassed by
this. Doesn't know what to do.*

### Three

*A Saturday afternoon, 15 May 2004, 5.30.*

*A bedroom in a B & B, Durham Road, Sunderland.*

**Jamie Carris** *is thirty-nine years old.*

*There is a big wooden table with two chairs on either side, two blue plates, a teapot, two blue teacups, an opened bottle of milk on it.*

*A big radio. A notebook and several different coloured pencils.*

*Window open to outside.*

**Jamie** *wears a blue shirt and jeans.*

*He has a cigarette in his hand. Unlit.*

**Emma Carris** *stands at the door. She is seventeen years old. She is wrapped in a big puffa-jacket coat. Her hair is wet, loose, shoulder-length.*

**Jamie**   Your hair's wet.

**Emma**   I had a shower. Before I came out.

**Jamie**   Would you like to come in?

**Emma**   Yeah. Yeah. Yeah. This is . . .

**Jamie**   What?

**Emma**   I don't know.

*He watches her come into his room.*

**Jamie**   Thank you for coming.

**Emma**   That's all right.

**Jamie**   I didn't know. You know. I didn't know what to think or what to say really or anything. It's good. I'm glad. Listen to me. Fucking going on. Sorry.

**Emma**   No. It's all right. Honest.

**Jamie**   Would you like a cup of tea?

**Emma**    Yes I would, please.

**Jamie**    Sit down. Sit down. Sit down.

*He moves a chair back for her to sit on. There are some papers on it.*

**Emma**    Thank you.

**Jamie**    Move the . . .

**Emma**    Yeah.

*She moves them onto the table. Sits. Doesn't take her coat off.*

**Jamie**    How would you like it?

**Emma**    Just milk.

**Jamie**    Right. Milk.

*He pours her cup of tea.*

Here we are.

*He watches her drink it.*

**Emma**    It's nice. Thank you.

**Jamie**    Would you like a cigarette?

**Emma**    No, thank you.

**Jamie**    No, right. Sorry. A sweet?

**Emma**    A what?

**Jamie**    Would you like a sweet?

**Emma**    A sweet? Go on.

*She laughs. Takes one. Doesn't open it.*

**Jamie** *opens his. Pops it in his mouth.*

**Jamie**    You can grow addicted to these. Mess your teeth up something terrible. Taste terrible with tea. Actually. I shouldn't have done that.

**Emma**    I'll save it.

**Jamie**    You found the place all right?

**Emma**    Yeah. It was easy.

**Jamie**    Was it?

**Emma**    Durham Road. Easy, that.

**Jamie**    Right. Good. That's good. You want to take your coat off?

**Emma**    No. I'm all right.

**Jamie**    You cold?

**Emma**    No. I'm fine.

**Jamie**    Not much, is it?

**Emma**    What?

**Jamie**    This place.

**Emma**    It's all right. I like it.

**Jamie**    Do yer?

**Emma**    Bit small. But –

**Jamie**    Yeah. Owner's all right. Bit weird. Very tall.

**Emma**    It's good round here.

**Jamie**    Is it?

**Emma**    Quite, y'know. Actually it's quite lively. Lots to do and that.

**Jamie**    Yeah. Yeah. Yeah. Yeah.

*Pause. He stares at her.*

Fucking hell, Emma.

**Emma**    What?

**Jamie**    Just . . . How old are you now?

**Emma**    Seventeen.

**Jamie**    Seventeen. Fucking. I don't believe that, me.

**Emma**    It's true. Honest.

**Jamie**    No. I know really. I'm just saying. (*Beat.*)
Whereabouts do you live?

**Emma**    Just up the road. In Tunstall.

**Jamie**    I've never been to Sunderland before.

**Emma**    Haven't you?

**Jamie**    No.

**Emma**    It's good. I like it.

**Jamie**    What's Tunstall like?

**Emma**    It's all right. It's quite nice.

**Jamie**    I thought it would be raining.

**Emma**    Did you?

**Jamie**    That's what you think, innit?

**Emma**    I don't know.

**Jamie**    That's what I thought.

**Emma**    It's not.

**Jamie**    No. It's all right.

**Emma**    What should I call you?

*Beat. He looks briefly away and then back. Smiles.*

**Jamie**    I don't know.

**Emma**    What do you think?

**Jamie**    Jamie. Maybe. Jamie's fine.

**Emma**    Jamie?

**Jamie**    Yeah.

**Emma**    Good. (*Beat.*) After you rang, I wanted to tell you something.

**Jamie**    Did yer?

**Emma**    Yeah. That's one of the reasons I came.

**Jamie**    Is it?

**Emma**    I'm not sure if I want to any more.

**Jamie**    OK.

**Emma**    I might. We'll wait and see.

*Pause, then* **Jamie** *leaps to his feet.*

**Jamie**    Can I show you something?

**Emma**    What?

**Jamie** *holds his sovereign ring in her face.*

**Jamie**    Here. Look at this. This ring. There's an engraving. Can you read that?

**Emma**    Yeah.

**Jamie**    I love that. Me.

**Emma**    It's very big, i'n't it? Shiny and that.

**Jamie**    Yeah. Yeah. It is. It.

*They look at each other for a bit and look away.* **Emma** *drinks her tea.*

**Emma**    I'm shaking. Look at me.

**Jamie** *doesn't know what to do and so they smile at each other.*

**Jamie**    You look different.

**Emma**    Do I?

**Jamie**    To how I thought you would. You look more.

**Emma**    What?

**Jamie**    You look older. You look lovely. Your clothes.
Way you dress. (*Beat.*) And you're?

**Emma**    What?

**Jamie**    You're working?

**Emma**    Yeah.

**Jamie**    A, a, a, a?

**Emma**    Receptionist.

**Jamie**    That's right. In a dentist?

**Emma**    Yeah.

**Jamie**    Fucking. That's a good job. That. Isn't it, though?
Do you enjoy it?

**Emma**    I love it, yeah.

**Jamie**    All them, all them, all them fucking people?

**Emma**    Yeah.

**Jamie**    With their teeth.

**Emma**    I know.

**Jamie**    That's. Amazing. I hate the dentist, me.

**Emma**    Why?

**Jamie**    Scares us.

**Emma**    Shouldn't. That's stupid.

**Jamie**    Yeah. Prob'ly. You think you're gonna stay there?
At the dentist's?

**Emma**    Yeah. I think so.

**Jamie**    That's good.

**Emma**    They've been saying. Could send us on courses.
Send us on a course. Train up. Computer skills. Office
management skills. Stick at it. Get the office manager's
position.

**Jamie**    Fucking hell.

**Emma**    What?

**Jamie**    Sorry, I shouldn't swear at you.

**Emma**    It's all right.

**Jamie**    Office manager. That's incredible to me.

**Emma**    Why?

**Jamie**    Just is. Just . . . I'm working.

**Emma**    Are you?

**Jamie**    In a garage. In Acton.

**Emma**    Where's Acton?

**Jamie**    In the west of London. I love it. You know. Cars. Pick 'em all apart. Look at 'em. Put 'em back together. I like all that. Makes yer think. Gaffer's all right. Bit of a wanker. Not too bad, though. Very quiet.

**Emma**    How long you been doing that?

**Jamie**    Since I got out. Six month now.

**Emma**    Six months?

**Jamie**    Mad, innit?

**Emma**    Yeah.

**Jamie**    So you must have been, at school and that, office manager! You must've been a right boffin.

**Emma**    A what?

**Jamie**    Right brainy.

**Emma**    No. Not really.

**Jamie**    Must've been, though.

**Emma**    I wasn't.

**Jamie**    Where did you go to school?

**Emma**    Just up our road. Thornhill.

**Jamie**    Was it all right? Was it?

**Emma**    Yeah. It was good. It was all right. I liked it. Glad I left.

**Jamie**    I hated school, me.

**Emma**    Did you?

**Jamie**    Wish I could, they should let. Be good to go now. You know what I mean?

**Emma**    You'd look a bit out of place.

**Jamie**    Yeah.

**Emma**    You'd look a bit fucking weird.

**Jamie**    I was always getting in bother.

**Emma**    Were yer?

**Jamie**    With the teachers. Give 'em jip like nothing. Fighting other kids. Kicking off. Tell yer. I was a right little cunt. (*Beat.*) Sorry.

**Emma**    I wasn't.

**Jamie**    Thamesview.

**Emma**    What?

**Jamie**    That was the name of it. Stupid name. See the river from all over Gravesend. There were Thamesviews fucking all over the place. Nothing special about the school. Fucking. Tell yer.

**Emma**    Right. This is a bit.

**Jamie**    I know.

*Pause.*

Are you all right?

**Emma**    Yeah. I am. I am. I'm. What's it like? Gravesend?

**Jamie**    It's all right. One whole side of it is the river. There's a big old bridge, up in Dartford which is a bit. I don't really go there much.

**Emma**    I sometimes think about it.

**Jamie**    Do you?

**Emma**    Like to see it, I think. Sometimes.

**Jamie**    Would yer?

**Emma**    Don't know.

*Pause. She looks at the papers she's moved.*

What you writing?

**Jamie**    What?

**Emma**    Your pad. What are you writing?

**Jamie**    I write the shipping forecast. I listen to it. On the radio. Write it down. Keep a chart. Just keep it recorded. Been doing it years. Started it inside.

**Emma**    Why?

**Jamie**    I don't know. Just 'cause. (*Beat.*) You must hate me.

**Emma**    No. Not hate.

*Pause.* **Jamie** *stands, moves away from the table. Goes over to the window. Looks out. Runs his hands behind his neck. Then turns to her.*

**Jamie**    Would you like to go out?

**Emma**    Out?

**Jamie**    Go out for a walk or something. We could. Or go and get a coffee. Or something like that.

**Emma**    No thank you.

**Jamie**    You could show us what it's like round here.

**Emma**    I don't think so.

**Jamie**    If it's good and that. Like you said.

**Emma**    No.

**Jamie**    Why not?

**Emma**    I don't really want to.

**Jamie**    Right. You want another cup of tea?

**Emma**    No, thank you.

**Jamie**    You sure?

**Emma**    I'll have my sweet now.

**Jamie**    Good idea.

*He watches her unwrap the sweet and start to chew it.*

How is it?

**Emma**    It's all right.

**Jamie**    Good. You sure you're all right in your coat and that?

**Emma**    I'm fine, yeah.

**Jamie**    Not hot?

**Emma**    No. No. No. No.

**Jamie** *looks at her eating her sweet.*

**Jamie**    Can I get a photograph of you?

**Emma**    You what?

**Jamie**    I don't have any photographs of you. Since you were a baby.

**Emma**    Right.

**Jamie**    I wanted to write to you. But that was a bit –

**Emma**    I don't know what photographs I've got. I don't really keep any photographs.

**Jamie**    No?

**Emma**    I can ask Mum.

**Jamie**   Yeah. That'd be. I'd like that. How is she? Your mum?

**Emma**   She's all right. She's well. Dad and that.

**Jamie**   I came to try and find you once.

**Emma**   Did yer?

**Jamie**   I had a day release. Tried to come up to Manchester. Didn't go too well.

**Emma**   No?

**Jamie**   No. Matty got your address for us and everything.

**Emma**   I remember Uncle Matty.

**Jamie**   Yeah?

**Emma**   I used to like him, I think. I think I used to think he was quite funny.

**Jamie**   Yeah. He still is.

**Emma**   What's he doing?

**Jamie**   He's married. He's, he's, he's thirty. Does a bit of chippying. Down Gravesend still. He's doing all right, y'know?

**Emma**   Yeah.

**Jamie**   I think it's great you're going to get more, do more training, get all that stuff. I think that's important. That makes me very proud of you.

**Emma**   Why?

**Jamie**   It just does. It's good to know things like that.

**Emma**   Right. I see.

**Jamie**   Should hear how you speak. Honestly. It's like.

**Emma**   What?

**Jamie**   Nothing. Look at you.

**Emma**    What?

**Jamie**    Your fucking, your hair and that!

**Emma**    What about it?

**Jamie**    It don't matter.

*Beat.*

**Emma**    Can I have a drink of water, please?

**Jamie**    Yeah. Yes. Yes. Yes. Of course you can.

*He fetches her a glass of water. He can't watch her drink it.*

**Emma**    You know one thing I remember about you?

**Jamie**    What?

**Emma**    I might have got this wrong.

**Jamie**    What?

**Emma**    When I was little, did I find a wasps' nest?

**Jamie**    Fucking hell.

**Emma**    I was tiny.

**Jamie**    That's right.

**Emma**    I remember that. I remember finding this thing, this, this, nest. Getting a big stick, I remember, and all these wasps come out of it. All I remember. I'm screaming. They're going in my mouth. And you come. And pick me up. And run with me. Is that right? Did this happen? Going to hospital with you. Both of us. Our skin all stung.

**Jamie**    You were about three.

**Emma**    I remember that.

**Jamie**    Emma.

**Emma**    What?

**Jamie**    –

**Emma**   What?

**Jamie**   I think it's good that you remember some things.

**Emma**   I don't remember much.

**Jamie**   No.

*He pulls a cigarette from the packet in his shirt pocket.*

Do you mind if I smoke this?

**Emma**   No.

**Jamie**   Are you sure?

**Emma**   Yeah.

**Jamie**   Should I open the window?

**Emma**   Yeah.

**Jamie** *does. Then turns and looks at her for a while.*

**Jamie**   Do you remember going to the park with us?

**Emma**   I'm not sure.

**Jamie**   I used to take you. Take you down the river. There's a park there. Little lake. Go on the swings and that. Give you a bit of a push. Play. Take you to the library sometimes. Get a book for you to look at. Looking at all the pictures and that. Take you on the ferry sometimes. We used to do that. Do you remember?

**Emma**   I don't think so.

**Jamie**   We did. I did. I used to do that. Did your mum not say?

**Emma**   No.

**Jamie**   Did she never tell you?

**Emma**   No. She didn't.

**Jamie**   When she took you up to Essex. You were, you must have been, I think, three. Maybe. She took you up

there. I used to come and see you. Weekends. Go over the
river. You used to come and meet us off the ferry
sometimes. That was where the wasps' nest was. A field. Just
behind your new flat. I remember all that.

**Emma**    I just remember feeling them in my mouth. It was
frightening.

**Jamie**    You must remember more than that, though.

**Emma**    I don't.

**Jamie**    You must, though, love.

**Emma**    I really don't. Honestly.

**Jamie** *clenches his fist and holds it behind his head.*

**Jamie**    When you was born. You was, like. You was a
breach. Is the word. And they had to do an operation.
I remember thinking what if anything happened to your
mum. And when you was a baby. The way your skin felt.
I've never felt anything. Your eyes. And all your, all your,
your hair.

**Emma**    Jamie.

**Jamie**    Yeah?

*No response.*

What?

**Emma**    You're starting to scare me a bit.

**Jamie**    To *scare* you?

**Emma**    Just a bit. Don't panic.

**Jamie**    Right. I'm –

**Emma**    I shouldn't be here, y'know?

**Jamie**    Why shouldn't you?

**Emma**    I never told Mum. I think she'd be a bit upset.

**Jamie**    She'd be fine.

**Emma**    I don't want to be too late.

**Jamie**    No. (*Beat.*) I remember the smell of you.

**Emma**    –

**Jamie**    And how I could, when you were crying, how I knew it was you.

**Emma**    Please don't do this.

**Jamie**    Do what?

**Emma**    I should probably go.

**Jamie**    Emma.

**Emma**    I did really want to see you, Jamie. I just wasn't expecting you to ring me up.

**Jamie**    I know.

**Emma**    I don't even know who you are or anything. And now I think –

**Jamie**    Emma.

**Emma**    I shouldn't have come. I was probably just being stupid. I don't know what you want me to do, or . . .

**Jamie**    I wanted to.

**Emma**    What?

**Jamie**    I wanted to see you.

**Emma**    Yeah, well, you've seen me now.

**Jamie**    Your gran's died.

**Emma**    I never knew her.

**Jamie**    Nearly ten years back. I was inside. They let us go out for the funeral.

**Emma**    I never knew her.

**Jamie**    When you were little my thing for you was I always wanted you to be better than her.

**Emma**    I never knew her. You might as well be talking Chinese to me.

**Jamie**    Don't say that.

**Emma**    You might.

**Jamie**    You remember coming to see us, in the nick?

**Emma**    No.

**Jamie**    You must do.

**Emma**    I don't, all right.

**Jamie**    The officers checked your socks. Made you take your socks off to look for, for, to look for.

**Emma**    I don't remember.

**Jamie**    Are you lying?

**Emma**    What?

**Jamie**    Are you?

**Emma**    No!

**Jamie**    You must be.

**Emma**    I'm going.

**Jamie**    Don't.

**Emma**    Shouldn't call people liars. I am. I'm leaving.

**Jamie**    Don't. Emma. Please. (*Beat.*) Please.

**Emma** *stops. Looks at him for some time. Bites her thumb. Looks away. Goes to the window. Looks out.*

**Emma**    You know when you rang us. I had something I wanted to tell you. Do you know what it was?

**Jamie**    No.

**Emma**    Were you on *Crimewatch*?

**Jamie**    You what?

**Emma** Were you? Mum told us. Said she went nuts. I'd throttle yer.

**Jamie** Yeah.

*Pause.* **Emma** *smiles at him. Looks out of the window. And then back.*

**Emma** You're not my dad. That was what I wanted to tell you. Not any more.

*Pause.*

I've got a dad. It's not you.

*Pause.*

I lied about you all the time. Until I was about. Ten. Maybe older. Then I stopped lying.

*Pause.*

Can I ask you a question?

**Jamie** Course.

**Emma** You killed somebody. Didn't yer?

**Jamie** What?

**Emma** Who was it?

**Jamie** It was a man called Ross Mack.

**Emma** Why did you do it?

*Pause.*

**Jamie** *looks at her, doesn't flinch.*

*He rubs his hand over the back of his head.*

**Jamie** It doesn't matter.

**Emma** Why, though?

**Jamie** It doesn't matter, really.

**Emma** What was it like?

**Jamie**  Don't.

**Emma**  What was it? Jamie? What was it like?

**Jamie**  I don't talk about this.

**Emma**  If you tell us, I'll stay.

**Jamie**  I wish I could go back in time. Turn my body back in time. Screw myself up into a, I don't know, a knot and go back and not do it. I have tried.

**Emma** *looks at him for a while.*

**Emma**  What was it like inside?

**Jamie**  I can't do this.

**Emma**  You've got to. If I've got to, you've got to. That's fair.

**Jamie** *looks back at her before he speaks. Raises his hand as if to touch her, even from a distance away. Can't. Lowers it again. Turns away.*

**Jamie**  When I left Wandsworth. Which was the last place I was at. Before I went to Latchmere House. There was a photograph, on the wall of the gate, of a prisoner who'd just been released. He was hanging around. Outside the nick. Following the screws. He couldn't leave it. Couldn't cope without it. (*Beat.*) Screws say to yer, when yer going, 'See yer soon.' (*Beat.*) When I come out. Just stood there. Couldn't move. Couldn't move my legs.

*Pause.*

I was so tired. On the way up here. Like when yer bones get tired.

*Pause.*

I want you to forgive me for the things that I've done.

**Emma**  To forgive you?

**Jamie**   I want you to forgive me for the things that I've done.

*Pause.*

I want you to forgive me for the things that I've done.

**Emma**   I know.

**Jamie**   I want you to.

**Emma**   I know.

**Jamie**   I want you to.

**Emma**   I don't know if I can.

**Jamie**   I never wanted to be separated from you. Not ever.

**Emma**   I know.

**Jamie**   I've wanted to see you every day. All the time.

**Emma**   That isn't my fault.

**Jamie**   I wanted so many things for you.

**Emma**   That doesn't mean anything.

**Jamie**   It does to me.

**Emma**   But it doesn't. Not really.

**Jamie**   As I get older. All I want now is things for you. For you to be safe. For you to have money and to be safe. And all the things that you want. For you to get them. Tell me one thing.

**Emma**   What?

**Jamie**   Tell me one thing that you want.

**Emma**   I can't think.

**Jamie**   Please tell me.

**Emma**   I'd like to fly a plane.

**Jamie**  I think that's brilliant, that. That stops me breathing.

*Pause. He goes to the window.*

Fucking. It's cold. Isn't it?

**Emma**  Yeah.

**Jamie**  I should close the window.

*He stands still for a bit. Then closes the window.*

*Very long pause. The two stand absolutely still.*

**Emma**  Can I go?

**Jamie**  What?

**Emma**  I want to go now.

**Jamie**  Right.

*He doesn't look back at her.*

**Emma**  Mum'll be wondering where I've got to.

**Jamie**  Right.

**Emma**  I'm not going to tell her.

**Jamie**  Right. I loved her more than I loved you. And that's . . .

*A slight pause.*

Sometimes I go out without a light for my cigarettes on purpose just so that I can ask somebody for a light. So that I can talk to them.

*A longer pause.*

**Emma**  When are you going home, Jamie?

**Jamie**  Tomorrow.

**Emma**  Right. Back to Acton?

**Jamie**    Yeah. (*Beat. Looking away from her.*) I want to hold your soul. In my hands. Cup it.

**Emma**    I don't know what that means.

**Jamie**    Would you like to see me again, one day? Would you like that, do you think?

**Emma**    I don't know.

**Jamie**    You could come down to Gravesend if you wanted to. One time. Doesn't need to be for a while.

**Emma**    I don't know.

**Jamie**    Have you ever been to Margate? I could take you to Margate. Would you like to go to Margate?

**Emma**    No. Maybe yeah. Probably not.

*Pause.*

*They stand still for a while yet.*

I should be going.

**Jamie**    I know. Yeah. I'm sorry.

**Emma**    Do I just close the door to behind me?

**Jamie**    What?

**Emma**    The latch, do I just pull it to behind me?

**Jamie**    Yeah. You do. That's. I won't come down with you.

**Emma**    No. I'm glad I've seen you.

**Jamie** *pulls a scrap of card from his pocket and a pen and writes a phone number.*

**Jamie**    Here. This is the number of the garage where I work. Will you ring us one day? When you're ready to?

**Emma** *takes the number.*

*Long pause.*

*She goes to the door.*

**Emma**  Thank you. I'll. Yeah. I'll. Bye, Jamie.

**Jamie**  Bye, love.

**Emma** *leaves.*

**Jamie** *sits at the table. Goes to kick it over. Can't.*

*Stares at it.*


**Four**

*Thursday 14 July 1983, 5.30 p.m.*

*Windmill Hill, Gravesend, Kent. A beautiful sunny day. Hot bright sky. There are the sounds of distant cars, birds.*

**Jamie Carris** *is eighteen. He is wearing work-clothes.* **Lynsey Sergeant** *is fifteen. She is wearing a school uniform. But only shirt, skirt, tie. Shirtsleeves rolled up. Shirt hanging out. Hair tied back off her face.*

*They lie on their backs, looking up at the clouds. He props his hand on his elbow, playing with his chest.*

*There is some time before they talk to one another.*

**Jamie** *starts to chuckle. Gets quite loud.*

**Lynsey**  Shhhh.

**Jamie**  What?

**Lynsey**  You. Calm down. It's all right now. It's quiet here. It's good.

*Pause.*

*She touches his arm, strokes it slightly, then points her hand up to one of the clouds.*

That one looks like an old man's face.

**Jamie**  Where?

**Lynsey**   There.

**Jamie**   Oh yeah. With a beard.

**Lynsey**   Ha!

**Jamie**   Jimmy Hill.

*Pause.*

I don't want to go work. Not now.

**Lynsey**   Don't then.

**Jamie**   I so don't want to.

*Pause.*

How long you got?

**Lynsey**   Not long. They'll start looking for us prob'ly. Are you sure you're all right?

**Jamie**   Yeah. Course. I'm glad you're here. Thank you for coming.

**Lynsey**   'S all right. Psycho.

*Pause.*

**Jamie**   She's a stupid cow. She's fucking mental. Just looks at us. I walked out.

**Lynsey**   What was he doing?

**Jamie**   She's sat on top of him. Skirt hitched up her arse. Fat cunt. Eyes rolling back in his head. Gary Noolan, for fuck's sake! I should go back and find him.

**Lynsey**   Fuck off.

**Jamie**   He'll be in the Station Arms. Bet yer. Should go and glass the cunt.

**Lynsey**   Don't, Jamie. Serious.

*Long pause.*

**Jamie**   I'm thirsty.

**Lynsey**    I'm hot.

**Jamie**    Yeah.

*Slight pause.* **Lynsey** *rolls over on her stomach to look at him.*
**Jamie** *doesn't look at her.*

**Lynsey**    Should take our tops off.

**Jamie**    Yeah.

**Lynsey**    Should do. No one'd see.

**Jamie**    Psycho.

**Lynsey**    Chicken.

*Chicken impersonations.* **Jamie** *chuckles.*

**Jamie** (*cod hard guy*)    Shut it.

*Long pause.*

I like you. (*Beat.*) You make us laugh.

**Lynsey**    Listen to you!

**Jamie**    What?

**Lynsey** (*imitating him*)    'I like you. You make us laugh.'

*She picks at the ground.*

You think Matty's dad knows? About your mum and
Noolan?

**Jamie**    Don't know.

**Lynsey**    What's he like, Matty's dad?

**Jamie**    Al? He's all right. Quiet. Don't mind him. Just sits
there most of the time.

*He snorts a half-laugh.*

*Long pause.*

How is school?

**Lynsey** (*suppressed laugh*)    Terrible.

*They burst out laughing.*

You know Mr Mackenzie?

**Jamie**   Yeah.

**Lynsey**   I bit him.

**Jamie**   You what?

**Lynsey**   Bit his hand. Bleeding and everything.

**Jamie**   You're fucking crackers, you.

**Lynsey**   I'm in Art, yeah? And Jones goes, 'Get out.' Sends us out. I ain't even done nothing. So I won't go. Start throwing things around. Paint and that.

**Jamie**   Why?

**Lynsey**   Just 'cause. He goes and gets Mackenzie and he grabs us round the waist. So I just bit him. Did his head.

**Jamie**   I bet.

**Lynsey**   Fucking going red. 'You BIT me!! You BIT me!!'

**Jamie**   Reckon he'll suspend you?

**Lynsey**   No. Hope so.

*Long pause.*

**Jamie**   How's Clarence House?

**Lynsey**   Same. You're better off at home.

**Jamie**   I'm gonna get you out.

**Lynsey**   Are yer?

**Jamie**   Yeah. Go back and get yer. Do a breakout. Come and stay at ours.

**Lynsey**   You reckon?

**Jamie**   I am. (*Beat.*) Be better if you were there. She wouldn't do my head in so much.

*Long pause.*

*Then* **Lynsey** *starts laughing.*

**Lynsey**   Guess what I'm thinking about.

**Jamie**   No.

**Lynsey**   Go on.

**Jamie**   No.

**Lynsey** (*drawling the name out like a child*)   Jamie.

**Jamie**   No.

**Lynsey**   Remember when I found yer?

**Jamie**   Yeah.

**Lynsey**   Fucking hanging there.

*She carries on laughing. He doesn't laugh.*

Got to admit it's quite funny.

**Jamie**   Idiot.

**Lynsey**   It is though. I'n't it? I'n't it funny? Spoilsport.

*Pause.*

You got any bruises?

**Jamie**   Yeah.

**Lynsey**   Still?

**Jamie**   Yeah.

**Lynsey**   Show us.

**Jamie** *pulls down his collar to reveal his neck.*

**Lynsey**   You looked mad.

**Jamie** (*smiling*)   Fuck off.

**Lynsey**   You seen mine?

**Jamie**   No.

**Lynsey** (*points to her thigh*)    Here?

**Jamie**    No.

**Lynsey** *pulls up her skirt to reveal the skin on her thigh.*

**Lynsey**    You really never seen this?

**Jamie**    No. How d'you get that?

**Lynsey**    When I was little I was climbing a tree. Fell. Got a branch through my leg. You wanna touch it? You can touch it.

**Jamie** *does.*

**Lynsey**    Don't feel nothing.

**Jamie**    It's rough. The skin.

**Lynsey**    Yeah.

**Jamie** *strokes it for a while. Then bends down and kisses the scar.*

**Lynsey** *smiles.*

*He leans over, slightly clumsily, and kisses her lips.*

*She smiles.*

*He moves away from her.*

*She leans back on her elbows. Smiles at him.*

**Lynsey**    That was nice. Don't need to stop, yer know?

**Jamie** *breaks away. Stands up.*

**Lynsey** *looks at him, trying to get inside his head.*

*He looks down at her.*

*She smiles. He looks away.*

*Pause.*

**Lynsey**    I should probably go.

**Jamie** (*turns to look at her*)    Don't.

**Lynsey**   I don't want to. I've got to. You know what they're like. They do their nut if I'm gone too long.

**Jamie** *looks away.*

**Jamie**   You wanna go for a drive later?

**Lynsey**   Maybe.

**Jamie**   Should I come round?

**Lynsey**   Yeah.

**Jamie** (*looks back*)   After I've been to the Station Arms? Found Gary Noolan?

**Lynsey**   Don't.

**Jamie**   I'm going to.

**Lynsey**   Jamie. I'm warning you.

**Jamie**   Are you?

**Lynsey**   Yeah.

**Jamie** (*looks right at her*)   Stay with us, then.

**Lynsey**   I can't.

**Jamie**   You can.

**Lynsey**   I want to get back.

**Jamie**   *Do* yer?

*Slight pause.*

**Lynsey** *can't reply.*

**Jamie** *looks away.*

**Jamie**   Al reckoned we was gonna go Margate.

**Lynsey**   When?

**Jamie**   All of us. Soon. You should come with us.

**Lynsey**   Yeah. Maybe. All right.

**Jamie** *looks up, right high up at the moon.* **Lynsey** *watches him. Laughs. Lies back down.*

*He puts his hands on his hips and smiles down at her.*

*Slow fade on the lights to black.*

# Motortown

*Motortown* was first performed at the Royal Court Jerwood Theatre Downstairs, London, on 21 April 2006. The cast was as follows:

| | |
|---|---|
| **Lee** | Tom Fisher |
| **Danny** | Daniel Mays |
| **Marley** | Daniela Denby-Ashe |
| **Tom** | Steve Hansell |
| **Paul** | Richard Graham |
| **Jade** | Ony Uhiara |
| **Justin** | Nick Sidi |
| **Helen** | Fenella Woolgar |

*Director*  Ramin Gray
*Lighting*  Jean Kalman
*Sound*  Ian Dickinson
*Choreography*  Hofesh Shechter

**Characters**

**Lee**
**Danny**
**Marley**
**Tom**
**Paul**
**Jade**
**Justin**
**Helen**

The play should be performed as far as possible without decor.

## One

**Danny** *and* **Lee**.

**Lee**   She doesn't want to see you. She told me to tell you.

*A brief pause.*

She told me to tell you that you were frightening her. Your letters were frightening, she said.

*A brief pause.*

I'm really, really, really, really sorry.

*A very, very long pause. The two brothers look at each other. Then* **Danny** *looks away. He moves away from* **Lee**.

**Lee**   You sleep all right?

**Danny**   I did. Thank you.

**Lee**   That's good.

**Danny**   I had some extraordinary dreams.

**Lee**   Did yer?

**Danny**   I did, yes.

**Lee**   What about?

**Danny**   I can't remember, to be honest. I say that. I'm not entirely sure if it's true. I'm not sure if it's that I can't remember or I can't quite believe them, yer with me? My dreams! I'm telling yer! What time is it?

**Lee**   It's nine o'clock. I've been up for a while. I was waiting for yer.

**Danny**   Were yer?

**Lee**   I get up at five thirty.

**Danny**   Do yer?

**Lee**   Most days.

**Danny**    Right. That's quite early, Lee.

**Lee**    Yes.

**Danny**    You should join the fucking army, mate.

**Lee**    Don't swear.

**Danny**    You what?

**Lee**    It's ignorant.

*Beat.*

**Danny**    That I was 'frightening' her? Are you sure that's what she said?

**Lee**    With your letters.

**Danny**    That's a bit of a surprise to me, I have to say.

*A pause.*

**Lee**    You sleep with a frown on your face. Did anybody ever tell you that?

**Danny**    No.

**Lee**    Well, it's true. I went in to check on you. You were frowning.

**Danny**    What have you been doing since half five?

**Lee**    I was cleaning the flat.

**Danny**    Good idea.

**Lee**    Can I get you some breakfast?

**Danny**    That'd be lovely, Lee. Thank you.

**Lee**    I've got some Coco Pops. Would you like some Coco Pops or would you prefer Sugar Puffs?

**Danny**    Coco Pops is fine.

**Lee**    And a cup of tea?

**Danny**    Lovely.

**Lee**   With milk and two sugars and the tea bag in first before the hot water?

**Danny**   That's right.

**Lee**   Would you like some toast as well?

**Danny**   I would, please.

**Lee**   I've got butter, margarine, Marmite, jam, marmalade, peanut butter, honey, Nutella and lemon curd.

**Danny**   Butter would be nice. And a little bit of marmalade please.

**Lee**   Right. Coming right up!

*He doesn't move.*

**Danny**   How've you been, Lee?

**Lee**   I've been all right. I've been very good. I've been healthy. I had to clean up quite quietly while you were sleeping. But that isn't a problem.

**Danny**   Good.

**Lee**   And how are you?

**Danny**   I'm fine, mate. I'm fine. It's nice to be back.

**Lee**   I should have asked if you wanted to sleep in my bed.

**Danny**   No, you shouldn't have done.

**Lee**   I should have done. I just chose not to.

I passed my driving test.

**Danny**   Nice one. Well done. When was that?

**Lee**   In January. It was easy. Passed first time.

**Danny**   I should think so. I did too.

**Lee**   Did you?

**Danny**   At Pirbright.

**Lee**   You didn't tell me.

**Danny**   We should get a car. Shouldn't we?

**Lee**   Yeah.

**Danny**   Put it in the driveway. Give it a clean. Show it off. You could wear a suit. Get a cup of tea in the morning. Go to work. With yer tie on. You'd love that, wouldn't you?

**Lee**   Ha!

**Danny**   How *are* Mum and Dad?

**Lee**   They're very well, thank you. I think they're pleased you're home.

**Danny**   Great.

**Lee**   They talk about you incessantly. It's like a kind of water torture for visitors.

**Danny**   I can imagine.

**Lee**   You gonna go and see them, you think?

**Danny**   I don't think so, no.

**Lee**   Right. Why?

**Danny**   I don't think I really want to, Lee, that's all.

**Lee**   I ironed your shirts for you. While you were sleeping. And after I tidied up.

**Danny**   Right. Thank you.

**Lee**   That's all right. I like ironing. I'm really good at it.

*He exits.*

**Danny** *stands alone. Long pause.*

**Lee** *returns with a cup of tea for both of them.*

**Danny**   Thanks, Lee. This is smashing.

**Lee**  We saw you on telly. On the news. On *Newsnight*. I went round to Mum and Dad's. They videotaped it. (*He drinks his tea.*) It didn't look anything like you.

**Danny**  I've not seen it.

**Lee**  Well, go round then. Ask Mum and Dad. They'd definitely let you watch it. You'll be astonished. It's like you're a completely different person.

**Danny** *eats, then looks at* **Lee**, *who is watching him.*

**Danny**  London?

**Lee** (*immediately*)    7,465,209.

**Danny**  Paris?

**Lee** (*immediately*)    2,144,703.

**Danny**  Mexico City?

**Lee** (*immediately*)    8,605,239.

**Danny** *gives him a big smile.* **Lee** *smiles back, proud and shy.*

**Lee**  Were you all right out there then, Danny?

**Danny**  I was, it was fine.

**Lee**  You spent most of your time giving out chocolates from what I could tell. They seemed quite friendly.

**Danny**  They were. See their little faces light up. All big grins. A mouthful of fucking Mars bar and they're putty in yer hand, Lee, I'm telling yer.

**Lee**  You're gonna be on *Trisha* soon, you. Knowing you. I think.

**Danny**  Fuck off.

**Lee**  'My addiction to swearing and being a swear monkey!'

**Danny**  When did she come round?

**Lee**   Last week.

**Danny**   Where's she staying?

**Lee**   Up Goresbrook, behind the field.

**Danny**   In her old house?

**Lee**   I think so, Danny, yes. But she told me not to tell you that.

**Danny**   Right.

**Lee**   She seemed very sure about it.

**Danny**   Yeah.

**Lee**   See Denise Van Outen?

**Danny**   Yeah. What about her?

**Lee**   I'd like to *be* her.

**Danny**   You what?

**Lee**   Just thinking out loud. How's your breakfast?

**Danny**   It's fine thank you, Lee. It's lovely.

**Lee**   Your hand's shaking.

**Danny**   Yeah.

**Lee**   It's always done that. What's that about, do you think?

**Danny**   I don't know.

**Lee**   West Ham got promoted.

**Danny**   I heard.

**Lee**   You missed it. And you missed my thirtieth birthday party.

**Danny**   I was at the camp.

**Lee**   It was a weekend. You stayed put. Watching *Grandstand*. I'm sorry about the Coco Pops. I feel like I've led you down the garden path. I've got no food in at all. I should have got some and I just didn't.

**Danny**   You still get your lunches?

**Lee**   Yeah.

**Danny**   They still bring them round?

**Lee**   Yeah. They do. Yeah.

**Danny**   Will they bring one round for me?

**Lee**   No. They won't.

Are you going to go out today, do you think?

**Danny**   I might do, Lee, yes.

**Lee**   I might go out today, too. After my lunch gets here.

**Danny**   We could fucking go out together.

**Lee**   I'm gonna start a swear box. I'll be able to buy a dishwasher by the end of it.

**Danny**   How much deodorant have you got on?

**Lee**   A bit.

**Danny**   Don't go fucking swimming, will yer?

**Lee**   Why?

**Danny**   You smell like a tart's boudoir!

**Lee**   Like a what?

**Danny**   Seriously. Show us yer teeth.

**Lee**   My teeth?

**Danny**   You wanna get them sorted, Lee, they're fucking disgusting. Here. Have a Polo. Have two. Have another, save it for later.

**Lee**   I told her she should tell you herself.

**Danny**  Did yer?

**Lee**  At first I did, but then I promised.

**Danny**  Thanks.

**Lee**  I didn't know what to do really.

**Danny**  Don't worry about it.

**Lee**  I never liked her anyway.

**Danny**  No.

**Lee**  The way she spoke to me. She was really rude.

*Pause.* **Danny** *smiles at him.*

**Danny**  We should go for a day trip. Us two, I think.

**Lee**  A day trip?

**Danny**  Go up Southend. Go to the seaside. Get a few drinks at the Northview. Look out to sea. Go and ride on the fairground. I'd look after you. See you all right. Be good that, I think. Don't you think, Lee, wouldn't you like that?

**Lee**  Maybe. After lunch.

**Danny**  I don't know if I can wait until lunchtime.

**Lee**  I have to, they're coming round.

*Pause.*

Are you incredibly angry with me, about Marley?

**Danny**  No, Lee, I'm not.

**Lee**  It's not my fault, is it?

**Danny**  No.

**Lee**  Don't shoot the messenger they say, don't they?

**Danny**  They do, yeah.

**Lee**  I'm glad you're a soldier.

**Danny**  Thanks.

**Lee**   I'm glad you're brave.

**Danny**   Thanks.

**Lee**   But you're incredibly messy.

**Danny** (*with a chuckle*)   Sorry.

**Lee**   Why are you laughing at me?

**Danny**   I just enjoy you. And I've not seen you.

**Lee**   I hate the summer. I get a bit sweaty.

**Danny**   You know the thing about you, Lee?

**Lee**   What?

**Danny**   You can kind of hold stuff in a bit. I quite admire that, as it goes.

**Lee**   That's not true.

**Danny**   It is, you know.

**Lee**   I can't hold anything in, me. I can't even hold my farts in.

**Danny**   That wasn't what I was talking about.

**Lee**   No.

**Danny**   I'm not going to wait until after lunch.

**Lee**   Right.

**Danny**   I think I'm going to go out on my own. Have a wander.

**Lee**   Will you be home for your tea?

**Danny**   I think so.

**Lee**   Give me a ring. On the phone. If you won't.

**Danny**   Right.

**Lee**   Are you going to go and see Marley?

**Danny**   No. Not if she doesn't want me to.

**Lee**   It's just what she says.

**Danny**   Yeah.

*He looks at* **Lee** *for a long time.*

**Danny**   Will you be here when I get back?

## Two

**Danny** *and* **Marley**.

**Danny**   Lee told me that you went to see him. He told me that you didn't want to see me any more. That you told him I was frightening you. Is that true, Marley?

*No response.*

Was I frightening you?

*No response.*

Was I frightening you, Marley? Were my letters frightening you?

**Marley**   Calm down.

**Danny**   I was writing you letters. They were letters, that's all.

**Marley**   Calm down, Danny, people are starting to stare at you.

**Danny**   Who is? Who's starting to stare at me?

**Marley**   There's no need to shout. I'm sitting right here.

**Danny**   If I was frightening you, then you could have told me yourself. You could have written to me. You could have come to see me. You didn't need to leave me a poxy message. I'm not sixteen any more.

**Marley**   –

**Danny**    I never wanted to frighten you. It was never my intention to frighten you.

**Marley**    All right.

**Danny**    I had nobody else I knew I could write to.

**Marley**    Fine.

**Danny**    Don't say that.

**Marley**    What?

**Danny**    Don't just sit there with your face screwed up like that. It's like you're passing a note through a classroom.

**Marley**    Danny, look, I'm glad you're back. I'm glad you're safe. I'm glad you didn't get your head blown off. I hope you're going to be OK.

**Danny**    I am.

**Marley**    But I don't owe you anything. And if I ask you to leave me alone, through your brother, or through a letter, or through a text message or a note via our teacher, then I expect you to leave me alone.

**Danny**    I'm gonna be more than all right. I'm gonna be great.

**Marley**    'Cause if you don't –

**Danny**    What?

**Marley**    I'll call the cops. I'll go to court. I'll get an order out on you, no danger.

**Danny**    You what?

**Marley**    I mean it, Danny.

*A long pause. He stares at her. She has to break his stare.*

Where you staying?

**Danny**    Where am I . . . ?

**Marley**    You heard me, where are you staying, Danny?

**Danny**    What do you wanna know that for?

**Marley**    You staying with your mum and dad?

**Danny**    No. I'm not. I'm staying at Lee's. What do you wanna know that for?

**Marley**    So I can tell the cops if you ever contact me again.

**Danny**    You're lying.

**Marley**    Try me.

**Danny**    You must be.

*A pause.* **Marley** *smiles.*

**Marley**    I saw your Lee a while back, as it goes. Having his driving lesson. Driving down the Heathway. He was driving at about twelve miles an hour. There was a big queue building up behind him.

**Danny**    Don't.

**Marley**    Why did you come and see me when I asked you not to?

**Danny**    Why do you think?

**Marley**    I have no idea.

*A very long pause.*

I'm gonna finish my tea.

**Danny**    Right.

**Marley**    And then I'm gonna go home.

*A very long pause. She drinks her tea.*

**Danny**    How is it?

**Marley**    What?

**Danny**    Your tea?

**Marley**    It's lovely.

**Danny**   That's good. Mine's a bit tepid. Should have tasted the tea we had out there. It was horrible.

**Marley**   I bet it was.

**Danny**   It was powdered.

**Marley**   Great!

**Danny**   It tasted like concrete.

**Marley**   Lovely.

**Danny**   I really missed you.

**Marley**   You said.

**Danny**   Is this going to be the last time I ever see you? 'Cause if it is I don't quite understand why.

**Marley**   Some of the things you said . . .

**Danny**   I don't remember.

**Marley**   I was only your girlfriend for about three months.

**Danny**   It was more than that.

**Marley**   And then you write that.

**Danny**   You have a way of talking to boys, did you know? It makes me want to smash their faces in.

*Pause. He grins.*

You got a boyfriend now?

**Marley**   Stop it.

**Danny**   Have you, Marley? Are you seeing somebody?

**Marley**   I don't believe this.

**Danny**   That means you have, doesn't it? Who is it, Marley? Who is he?

**Marley**   I'm going.

**Danny**   Marley, who is he? Do I know him?

**Marley**    See you, Danny.

**Danny**    Did he go to our sixth form?

**Marley**    Fuck off.

**Danny**    Don't. Don't, Marley. Please don't.

*He goes to her. Grabs her arm.*

**Marley**    Get off my arm.

*He lets go of her.*

**Danny**    Please don't go.

**Marley**    Fuck off.

**Danny**    Please, Marley, don't. I'm sorry. I just missed you, is all. If that's out of order then I take it all back.

**Marley**    I stopped being your girlfriend years ago.

**Danny**    It wasn't years.

**Marley**    I thought you were my friend.

**Danny**    Yeah.

**Marley**    There's nothing wrong with that. I was going to university. You were down in Pirbright. I thought we were mates.

**Danny**    Yeah. I know.

**Marley**    Your letters were really weird and they were really frightening. You really hurt my arm.

**Danny**    I'm sorry.

*A very long pause.*

I wish you'd come. To Pirbright. To see me. It was an amazing place. Better than anywhere round here by miles. I wish you'd come to the passing out. Lee came. He was an embarrassment. With his big old glasses on. Looking like a freak.

**Marley**    How long you gonna stay with him?

**Danny**    Not long.

**Marley**    Where are you gonna move to?

**Danny**    I have no idea.

**Marley**    Don't they sort you out with somewhere?

**Danny**    No. I paid myself out.

**Marley**    So they just leave you?

**Danny**    They do, yeah.

**Marley**    To fend for yourself?

**Danny**    Yeah.

**Marley**    Well, you should be good at that, shouldn't you? You're trained for that, aren't you, Danny? You could go to the Marshes. Dig a hole.

**Danny**    I could, yeah.

**Marley**    You'd love that, you, I bet.

**Danny**    I can lie awake at night and imagine what it's like to kiss your face.

**Marley**    Don't.

**Danny**    You can too, I bet.

**Marley**    This is ridiculous. You couldn't even get it up half the time. Could you, though? When you think about it. Came in about two seconds when you did.


**Three**

**Danny** *and* **Tom.**

**Tom**    I think people are more like flowers than we ever give them credit for.

**Danny**    You what?

**Tom**    See me, Danny. I'm a little flower. Bit of sunshine like this and I bloom, mate. Get outside. Put yer shorts on. You wanna do a bit of that.

**Danny**    You reckon?

**Tom**    I didn't think they'd let you out yet, Danny.

**Danny**    Didn't yer?

**Tom**    I thought you'd still be out there.

**Danny**    I came home early.

**Tom**    You had enough, had you?

**Danny**    I had, a bit.

**Tom**    How was it?

**Danny**    It was easy.

**Tom**    Pushing on an open door.

**Danny**    Mostly it involved waiting around all fucking day. Do a couple of patrols.

**Tom**    Give out a few Spangles.

**Danny**    We stayed in the airport. They turned the Basra international airport into our base. Had these big old statues and fountains and marble floors and everything.

**Tom**    Lovely.

**Danny**    Had a PlayStation. Watch a few DVDs. Get yer one ginger beer a day.

I just got bored.

Came home.

*Beat.*

*They smile at each other.*

**Tom**    I'm glad you did.

**Danny**    Me too.

**Tom**   It's good to see yer.

**Danny**   Yeah. It's good to see you, too.

**Tom**   You want a crisp, Danny? They're sea salt and malt vinegar.

**Danny**   Lovely. Thank you.

**Tom** *looks at* **Danny** *for a long time.*

**Tom**   You staying with your Lee?

**Danny**   I am, yeah.

**Tom**   How is he, Lee?

**Danny**   He's fucking completely puddled. But he's not so bad. I quite like him. I'm on his couch.

**Tom**   Nice. You not going see your folks?

**Danny**   I don't think so, Tom, no.

**Tom**   They still up in Becontree, are they?

**Danny**   They are, mate, yeah.

**Tom**   How come you're not gonna go and see them?

**Danny**   'Cause they do my fucking head in, Tom.

**Tom**   Do they?

**Danny**   They do, yeah.

**Tom**   Right. Right. Right. Right. Good. And have you seen Marley?

**Danny**   I haven't, Tom, no.

**Tom**   Best off out of that one, I reckon.

**Danny**   Yeah, me too.

**Tom**   I think she was completely insane.

**Danny**   I think you're right.

**Tom**   I saw you on the telly. With Paxo. I thought you looked all right. I thought you came off fairly well, as it goes.

**Danny**   Thanks, Tom.

**Tom**   Other people said they thought you looked a bit odd.

**Danny**   Did they?

**Tom**   Said it looked nothing like you. Are you as hard as fuck now?

**Danny**   You what?

**Tom**   Are you?

**Danny**   I don't know. I don't think so.

**Tom**   You look it, you know?

**Danny**   Thanks, Tom.

**Tom**   You look quite handsome, as it goes.

**Danny**   That's very kind of you.

**Tom**   In a kind of James Cagney kind of way.

**Danny**   James Cagney?

**Tom**   Definitely more James Cagney than Leonardo DiCaprio. What are you gonna do for money?

**Danny**   I'm all right for a bit.

**Tom**   You could come and work here, if you wanted.

**Danny**   Thanks, Tom. I'll be fine.

**Tom**   Work on the till. Count the cash. Place the orders. Any of that.

**Danny**   That's kind of you, mate.

**Tom**   And have you got long-term plans?

**Danny**   Not completely, no.

**Tom**   I think you should look into a career in film special effects.

**Danny**   Do yer?

**Tom**   You'd be good at that, I think.

**Danny**   You reckon?

**Tom**   I do, yeah.

**Danny**   How much is this, Tom?

**Tom**   Thirty-five pounds. I could give it you for twenty-seven.

**Danny**   Thank you.

**Tom**   That's not a problem. You're a friend of mine. I'm happy to help you out.

It's a Walther P99 replica. Semi-automatic. There's no hammer, see? The trigger's beautiful, I think. Although it is odd at first. It has a very long, double-action first shot. But then it's very clean, for the rest of the magazine. You don't need to exert any pressure at all. It has a six-millimetre calibre. It takes 0.2 gram pellets. I can *give* you a hundred of those as part of the deal. It's a very authentic model, this one. Probably the most authentic I've got in just now.

**Danny**   Right.

**Tom**   I've got a good deal on the Smith & Wesson at the moment. Which is a simple six-shot. At twenty pounds. I've got a Taurus PT92 in chrome, which I think is actually rather elegant. That's thirty pounds to you. I've got a KWC Beretta for you at fifteen quid, Danny. 0.12 gram pellets, nearly hundred metres a second. If you fancy it we could take them out.

**Danny**   Nice one.

**Tom**   Go up home. Go up the Chase. Shoot some ducks.

**Danny**   We could do.

**Tom**   Mind you, you could probably get us on Foulness, couldn't you? Get on the Island.

**Danny**   I could try.

**Tom**   You ever been up there?

**Danny**   I haven't, Tom, no.

**Tom**   I'd fucking love to go there, me.

**Danny**   Yeah. I'll take this, Tom.

**Tom**   Good choice.

**Danny**   It's a good weight, eh?

**Tom**   It's a cop gun. Special forces. Undercover. James Bond type of thing.

**Danny**   Great.

**Tom**   You got cash?

**Danny**   I do, yeah.

**Tom**   Lovely.

**Danny**   I've not been up the Chase since I've got back.

**Tom**   I've not been for fucking years, mate.

**Danny**   It's changed, hasn't it? The whole town.

**Tom**   I can never tell any more.

**Danny**   It has, it's got worse, I think.

**Tom**   The factory's almost completely closed up now.

**Danny**   I heard. I went down. To get the train up here.

**Tom**   The whole of Chequers is all completely burnt out. All of it. The whole fucking street.

**Danny**   Yeah.

**Tom**    There's a whole new array of drugs you can get down there. Drugs I've never even heard of before. It's like a supermarket for drugs.

**Danny**    I'm half tempted to go up Eastbrook.

**Tom**    Are you?

**Danny**    Take this with me. 'All right, sir?' Bang!

**Tom**    Ha! Don't.

**Danny**    No. Don't worry, I won't.

**Tom**    I know what we should do!

**Danny**    What's that?

**Tom**    We should go up Shoeburyness. Take my car up. Do some doughnuts. I've not done that since you left. Or go Southend. Go cockle picking.

**Danny**    Yeah.

**Tom**    Have you got the new 50 Cent album?

**Danny**    I haven't, Tom, no.

**Tom**    It's fucking great.

**Danny**    Is it?

**Tom**    What about the new Outcast?

**Danny**    No.

**Tom**    Snoop Dog?

**Danny**    I've not.

**Tom**    Black Eyed Peas?

**Danny**    No.

**Tom**    I've got all of them. Jay-Z, featuring Beyoncé?

**Danny**    No.

**Tom**    He's a lucky cunt, isn't he?

**Danny**   He is, yeah.

**Tom**   I'll burn 'em for you! Have you got an iPod?

**Danny**   No.

**Tom**   You should get one, I think.

**Danny**   Yeah, I will.

**Tom**   I've got 6,324 songs on mine. Mostly hip hop. I got some Rod Stewart, for me mum.

**Danny**   If I wanted it converted, would you know where I could go?

**Tom**   Sorry, Danny?

**Danny**   The P99, if I wanted it engineered, to fire live ammo, do you know anybody who could do that for me?


**Four**

**Danny**, **Paul** *and* **Jade**.

**Paul**   To ask about the meaning of life is about as philosophically interesting as asking about the meaning of wood or the meaning of grass. There is no meaning. Life is, as science has proven in the last two years, a genetic system. An arrangement of molecular structure. There is no solidity. Only a perception of solidity. There is no substance. Only the perception of substance. There is no space. Only the perception of space. This is a freeing thing, in many ways, Danny. It means I can be anywhere. At any time. I can do anything. I just need to really try. This is Jade. Say hello, Jade.

**Jade**   Hello.

**Danny**   Hello.

**Paul**   How's Tom doing?

**Danny**   He's all right, I think.

**Paul**    Good man. Good man. Good man. He's a bit of a weird old cunt though, don't you think?

**Danny**    I do, sometimes.

**Paul**    He is. He speaks very highly of you, but he is a bit of a weird old cunt.

**Danny** (*to* **Jade**, *lying*)    Jade was my wife's name.

**Paul**    Are you married, Danny?

**Danny**    I was.

**Paul**    How old are you?

**Danny**    Twenty-seven.

**Paul**    What happened to your wife, Danny?

**Danny**    She got killed.

**Paul**    No.

**Danny**    We got robbed. She got shot in the chest.

**Paul**    Good God, Danny, that's awful.

**Danny**    Yeah.

**Paul**    When was this?

**Danny**    A couple of years ago.

**Paul**    Did they catch the fucker?

**Danny**    Yeah. He was a soldier. Some squaddie.

**Paul**    For God's sake. I'm really sorry to hear that. Aren't you, Jade? Aren't you sorry to hear that?

**Jade**    Yeah. I am.

**Paul**    We're both of us really sorry to hear that, Danny.

*A long pause.*

Yes.

Is it Danny or Daniel?

**Danny**   Danny.

**Paul**   Good. How boyish! What do you do, Danny?

**Danny**   What do I do?

**Paul**   Your job, what is it?

**Danny**   I'm in film. I do special effects for films.

**Paul**   Do you really? That's rather remarkable to me!
What a remarkable job. What films have you done?

**Danny**   None that you know.

**Paul**   Go on. Try me. I go to the cinema all the time,
don't I, Jade?

**Jade**   Yeah. He does.

**Danny**   I worked on a few of the Bond movies. I worked
on the gun scenes on some of the Bond films.

**Paul**   Which ones?

**Danny**   *Die Another Day*. Mainly.

**Paul**   I never saw that. Did I?

**Jade**   No.

**Paul**   I hate James Bond. I think his films are fucking
dreadful. Did you come in on the train?

**Danny**   I did, yeah.

**Paul**   I like the train ride. Out of Dagenham.

**Danny**   Yeah.

**Paul**   I like Dagenham.

**Danny**   Do yer?

**Paul**   It's full of fat kids in football shirts, isn't it? Lovely
that. I like it round here more, though. I like the views, you
understand?

**Danny**   I do.

**Paul**   Canning Town. London, E16. Do you like London, Danny?

**Danny**   I'm not sure.

**Paul**   You're not sure?!

**Danny**   It's a bit big for me.

**Paul**   A bit big. (*He smiles.*) You see, that's the problem with the Essex native, though, Danny, isn't it? They never fucking leave.

**Danny**   That's not completely true.

**Paul**   What's the furthest you've ever been to?

**Danny**   You what?

**Paul**   In the world?

**Danny**   France.

**Paul**   Is it?

**Danny**   Yeah.

**Paul**   Ha!

**Jade** *smirks too.*

**Danny**   Don't laugh.

**Paul**   No. You're right. I'm being rude. I'm sorry. It's just I'm quite the traveller. I travel almost constantly. I'm more familiar with aeroplanes than I am with buses. That's actually the truth. Do you want to know something about aeroplanes?

**Danny**   Go on.

**Paul**   You know the real reason why people tell you to adopt the brace position in the event of an emergency on an aeroplane? It's so the impact of the crash on the neck forces the spinal column into the skull and into the brain and kills you immediately. Rather than allowing you to suffer a prolonged and horrible death. That's the reason why, really.

**Danny**  This is my gun.

*He pulls his gun out of his pocket and shows it to him.*

**Paul**  Yes. Put it away. We'll sort that out in a bit. Can I get you a cup of tea, Danny?

**Danny**  No thank you.

**Paul**  Or a coffee? Or a beer? A whisky? Anything like that?

**Danny**  A water.

**Paul**  A water? You want a glass of water? Tap or mineral?

**Danny**  Tap.

**Paul**  Tap water. Very good. Ice? Lemon?

**Danny**  No thank you.

**Paul**  As it comes, as it were. Terrific. Jade, sweetheart, get Danny a glass of water, will you? There's a good girl.

**Jade** *leaves. They watch her go.*

**Paul**  She's fourteen. You wouldn't think it to look at her, would yer?

**Danny**  I don't know.

**Paul**  You wouldn't. Immoral really, but . . .

*A long pause.* **Paul** *stares at* **Danny**.

**Paul**  Can I ask you this? Do you ever get that feeling? When you're in, you're in, you're in say a, a, a, a bar or a restaurant or walking down a street, and you see a girl. A teenage girl. You see the nape of her neck. In her school uniform. With her friends. All pigtailed. And you just want to reach out and touch. You ever get that?

**Danny**  I'm not sure.

**Paul**   You see, when you can't tell the difference any more between what is real and what is a fantasy. That's frightening, I think.

They don't let you take anything onto planes any more, Danny. Did you know that? Since 9/11. Fucking nothing. Apart from pens, oddly. They should take pens off you. That's what I think. The pen can be a lethal instrument. You can stab somebody in the eye. Push it all the way in. Cripple them at least. Cut into the brain. Leave them brain-damaged. It'd be easy, that. I'd leave the end sticking out, wouldn't you?

**Danny**   I don't know.

**Paul**   You would. I would. It would look hilarious.

I need a shave.

You know what I think about 9/11, Danny?

**Danny**   No, I'm actually in a bit of a –

**Paul**   Wait for your fucking drink!

**Danny**   –

**Paul** *glares at him.*

**Paul**   The best heist film Hollywood never made. That's what I think. The level of planning, the level of daring, the downright fucking scientific sexiness and brass-balled braveness that went into that operation! Christ! You should tell your friends. They could cast it up! Cast Bruce Willis. Black him up a bit. That'd be a fucking blockbuster all right.

**Danny**   Yeah.

**Paul**   They should make films out of everything, I think. Films and musicals. They should make musicals out of everything as well. Imagine it! *Bulger! The Musical!* I'd pay forty quid to see that.

**Jade** *returns. She gives* **Danny** *a glass of water.*

**Danny**   Thank you very much.

**Jade**   That's all right.

**Paul** *waits for* **Danny** *to drink. Watches him.*

**Paul**   How is it? Your water?

**Danny**   It's fine, thanks.

**Paul**   Look out there. Have you the slightest idea how many tube lines run under the square mile area you can see from out of that window, Danny, have you? It's completely fucking hollow down there. Beneath the surface of the ground. It's full of vermin and metal. Rats. Mice. Squirrels. Foxes. Soon there'll be dogs fucking everywhere. Stray dogs. Little pit bulls. Wandering around. They'll come in down the river. And then, in the future, in London, people will find foxes in their living rooms. You'll have to batter them with your broomsticks. Or shoot them in the head. Either method works just as well. Scabby fucking things. They'll eat your cat as soon as look at you. I'm gonna bring hunting for foxes with hounds back. But not in fucking Surrey. Not in Wiltshire. Down Oxford Street. A huge fucking pack of us.

*He makes the noise of a hunting trumpet.*

Show me.

**Danny** *shows him his gun.*

**Paul**   P99. Nice. Let me have a look.

*He opens a small toolkit, takes out a tiny screwdriver and a tape measure and opens the gun. Goes to work adjusting it. He wears half-moon spectacles as he does so.*

The notion of a War on Terror is completely ingenious. It is now possible to declare war on an abstraction. On an emotional state.

*He continues to work.*

God. Law. Money. The left. The right. The Church. The
state. All of them lie in tatters. Wouldn't you be frightened?

*He continues to work.*

The only thing we can do is feast ourselves on comfort foods
and gobble up television images. Sport has never been more
important. The family unit seems like an act of belligerence.
*All* long-term relationships are doomed or ironic. Therefore
sexuality must be detached. But detached sexuality is
suicidal. So everybody goes online.

Hardcore black fucking MPEG porn . . . junky lesbian
breast torture . . . bondage fantasies, hardcore pics . . . free
bestiality stories, low-fat diet, free horse-sex, torture victims
zoo . . .

Marvellous stuff!

You can get all the free trailers. And that's enough for me.
I wouldn't spend any fucking money on it. That's just a
waste, I think. I think that's when you're addicted to it.

*He continues to work.*

I saw a fifty-year-old man sit a sixteen-year-old Brummie
girl on his lap. He held her breast in his hand and got her to
smile at the webcam. Asked her what she thought all of the
people watching did while she masturbated. She said she
thought they masturbated. It was a truthful image. It sits in
my consciousness.

*He looks up at* **Danny** *and points with his tiny screwdriver.*

**Paul**    You want to know the truth about the poor in this
country? They're not cool. They're not soulful. They're not
honest. They're not the salt of the fucking earth. They're
thick. They're myopic. They're violent. They're drunk most
of the time. They like shit music. They wear shit clothes.
They tell shit jokes. They're racist, most of them, and
homophobic the lot of them. They have tiny parameters of
possibility and a minuscule spirit of enquiry or investigation.
They would be better off staying in their little holes and

fucking each other. And killing each other. And the girls are so vapid. You know the type? All brown skin and puppy fat and distressed denim on their arses and ponchos.

*He continues to work.*

When Jade's gone I think I'm going to start spending my time in the bars of Borough Market. Or Sloane Street. Or Bloomsbury. Get myself a rich girl, a business girl. You see them. And below their suits and their handbags and their fresh, fresh skin and clean hair, you know, you just fucking know.

Royalty are the worst, of course. Mind you, if I was the king of this country I'd start every morning with a blow job too. From my butler. With my coffee and my yogurt and my fruit. It's the most civilised thing I can imagine. It's absolutely legendary.

Wait here.

*He leaves.* **Danny** *drinks his water.* **Jade** *shifts her position. He looks at her.*

**Danny**　Will he be long?

**Jade**　I don't know.

*Pause.*

**Danny**　Doesn't he do your head in after a while?

**Jade**　What do you mean?

**Danny**　He goes on a bit, doesn't he?

**Jade**　I like him.

**Danny**　Is he your boyfriend?

**Jade**　Ha!

**Danny**　What's funny?

**Jade**　'Is he your boyfriend?'

**Danny**　What's funny about that?

**Jade**   Nothing. It doesn't matter.

**Danny**   You shouldn't laugh at people. Shouldn't laugh at me, definitely. Shouldn't you be at school?

**Jade**   I don't go to school any more.

**Danny**   Why not?

**Jade**   It's boring. I don't need to, anyway. Paul teaches me all kinds of stuff.

**Danny**   I can imagine.

I used to go Eastbrook. In Dagenham. You ever heard of it?

**Jade**   No.

**Danny**   It's a fucking remarkable place. For a thousand reasons. But I never really felt completely comfortable there, you with me?

**Jade**   –

**Danny**   I always wanted to go out. See, you'd get a day like this. Go down the docks. Fuck that lot. Go and watch the river. Go over the Chase. Don't you think, Jade?

**Jade**   –

**Danny**   Have a day trip. We should have a day trip. Us two. Me and you, Jade. What do you think?

**Jade**   I don't think Paul would like it.

**Danny**   He wouldn't mind. Would he?

**Paul** *comes back in with the gun complete.*

**Danny**   Would you, Paul? Would you mind if I took Jade for a day trip? Hop in the car. Go to the seaside.

**Paul** *looks at him for a long time. Hands him back his gun.*

**Paul**   Do you need ammunition?

**Danny**   I do, yeah.

**Paul**   Here. 125 gram, nine-millimetre standard pressure
hollow-point. Fifty rounds, ten pounds. Sixty pounds total.
That's a very good price.

**Danny**   Thank you.

**Paul** *hands him a small, plain, red box.* **Danny** *hands him sixty
pounds. He examines his gun with a confidence and proficiency that
belies the notion that he is anything other than a soldier.*

**Paul**   This weather.

**Danny**   Yeah.

**Paul**   This whole planet is in a terrible state, Danny, you
know? The ecological fallout of the decisions that you have
made – you, Danny, personally, today, you, not anybody else,
you – the ecological fallout of those decisions is catastrophic.
And it's the same for all of us. Times sixty million. Times six
billion. And nobody says anything about it. There are too
many people. There is not enough water. There is not enough
oxygen. And nobody admits it. And so now we're gonna
consume China. And then we're gonna consume India and
then we're gonna consume Africa and we'll carry on
consuming. We'll continue to eat it all up and eat it all up
and eat it all up until the only thing we've got left to fucking
eat, Danny, the only thing we've got left to eat is each other.

**Five**

**Danny** *and* **Marley**.

**Danny**   We could get a car. Get a nice one. CD player.
Seat belts. Airbags. All that. A really silent one. Get a couple
of kids. Drive them to school. Nip off to work in yer suit. See
you later, Danny. See you later, Lee! Have a good day,
boys. Do all that.

**Marley**   Danny.

**Danny**   Are you cold?

**Marley**    What are you doing here?

**Danny**    I got something for yer.

**Marley**    You can't come round here any more.

**Danny**    You could make us all a cup of tea in the morning. We could buy a fucking Teasmade! You'd be in for Danny and Lee when they got home from school. I'd be at work but get home later and watch the news!

**Marley**    This is stupid.

**Danny**    Do you remember my flat?

**Marley**    –

**Danny**    It was good there, wasn't it? I wish I never sold it. I've nowhere to go now.

**Marley**    Danny, you're shaking. I'm gonna call your brother.

**Danny**    I'll tell you something. The amount of fucking snatch I'm gonna get now, Marley, you wouldn't believe.

**Marley**    The amount of what?

**Danny**    I already met somebody. We're going on a date. Jade, she's called. Black girl. A fucking coon. How d'yer like that?

**Marley**    Don't, Danny.

**Danny**    Don't what?

**Marley**    It's boring.

**Danny**    You know how old she is?

**Marley**    –

**Danny**    Have a guess.

**Marley**    No.

**Danny**    She's forty-three.

**Marley**   Great.

**Danny**   That's the level I'm pitching it at nowadays.

**Marley**   Lovely.

**Danny**   Did you see me on the telly, by the way?

**Marley**   I didn't, no.

**Danny**   I was fucking brilliant. Made fucking Paxo look like . . .

**Marley**   That's not what I heard.

**Danny**   You what?

**Marley**   I heard you could barely speak. Didn't look anything like you. You look terrible, Danny. What have you been doing?

**Danny**   I've been at my folks, all day, really.

**Marley**   How they doing?

**Danny**   They're doing all right. They're well. I mean, I hate them so it's difficult for me to tell.

**Marley**   You hate them?

**Danny**   I do a bit. My dad mainly. Drunken fucking contradictory wanker. I find him completely ridiculous. I hope I get to bury him.

*She looks at him for a long time.*

What are you thinking?

**Marley**   Are you gonna go up London soon? And look at things?

**Danny**   What do you mean?

**Marley**   All the tourist attractions. You used to go, do you remember? Stand outside them. Looking in.

*Pause. He glares at her. Then grins.*

**Danny**   When I've finished with you I'm going to go and find every boyfriend you ever had and every friend you ever had and get them and shoot them in the face.

**Marley**   You what?

**Danny**   And all your family.

**Marley**   That's nice, Danny.

**Danny**   Do you think I won't, Marley, do you think I wouldn't? This is what I'm trained to do.

**Marley**   I think you need to go to the hospital.

**Danny**   I've got something for you. I went out, into town, up London, this afternoon and got a present for you. I've not decided whether you're gonna get it yet.

**Marley**   A present?

**Danny**   I don't know if you'll like it or not. You probably won't.

**Marley**   What are you like, Danny? Jesus!

**Danny**   You look quite sexy when you get angry.

**Marley**   I'm going now.

**Danny**   What about your present?

**Marley**   I don't want your poxy present. What is it? Box of chocolates, is it? Box of Black Magic?

You should know. I wanted to tell you. I do have a boyfriend. I've been seeing him for years. We're gonna get married, I think. We're gonna have kids. I'm gonna be a mum to his kids.

*He can't look at her.*

All you ever do is talk and talk and talk.

I can't do this any more. It does me no good.

**Danny**   –

**Marley**   You're shivering.

**Danny**   I'm sorry.

**Marley**   What are you sorry for?

**Danny**   It's not me. It isn't me.

**Marley**   What isn't you? Fucking hell!

**Danny**   I'm really sorry.

**Marley**   I wanted to be your mate. I wanted to come round for tea and fags and biscuits.

**Danny**   I don't think so. Not now. No.

Marley.

**Marley**   What?

**Danny**   Marley.

**Marley**   Are you crying?

**Danny**   Marley.

**Marley**   What, Danny? Jesus!

**Danny**   Go back in. You should go back inside. I don't think I should see you any more.


**Six**

**Danny** *and* **Jade**.

**Danny**   It's lovely here, isn't it?

**Jade**   –

**Danny**   Most people don't even know this place exists. Some maps don't even show the road onto it.

See his face, on the checkpoint, when I showed him my pass. That was a bit of a surprise for him, I think. What do you think?

**Jade**   I don't know.

**Danny**   Sorry?

**Jade**   I said I don't know.

**Danny**   It was, I think. I think it was a big surprise.
Uptight cunt. Officer class. Failed.

**Jade**   What are you gonna do?

**Danny**   See miles from here and all, can't you? See
France, I reckon, on a good day.

**Jade**   Are you gonna hurt me?

**Danny**   Or Holland. What do you think, Jade? Do you
reckon you could see Holland from here?

**Jade**   I don't know.

**Danny**   Do you think he'll notice you've gone – Paul?

**Jade**   Yeah.

**Danny**   Do you?

**Jade**   Yes, I do.

**Danny**   Do you think you were very important to him?

**Jade**   Yes.

**Danny**   Do you think he was a bit in love with you, Jade?

**Jade**   I don't know.

**Danny**   You looked very funny when I turned up. Did you
get the fright of your life?

**Jade**   I did a bit.

**Danny**   Did you?

**Jade**   Yeah.

**Danny** (*as though to a cute puppy*)    Aaahhh.

*A pause. He moves away from her. Looks out to sea.*

Were you good at school?

**Jade**    What?

**Danny**    When you went to school, Jade, were you quite good at it?

**Jade**    Yeah.

**Danny**    I bet you were. You look as though you were. You're quite confident, aren't you? Did you *ever* like it?

**Jade**    Yeah.

**Danny**    When did you enjoy it?

**Jade**    In primary school. Year seven was all right.

**Danny**    And then it all went a bit wrong for you?

**Jade**    –

**Danny**    Would you ever go back, do you think? Go sixth form?

**Jade**    I think so, yeah.

**Danny**    'Cause you're quite brainy, aren't you? For your age?

**Jade**    I don't know.

**Danny**    What would you do if you did?

**Jade**    I'm not sure.

**Danny**    What A levels would you take?

**Jade**    I –

*She starts crying a bit.*

**Danny**    Well, that's clever. You're gonna stay on at sixth form but you don't know what you're going to study there.

**Jade**    I haven't decided.

**Danny**    See, that's the fucking thing, isn't it? Nowadays. Young people today! They have no idea what they're going to fucking *do* with their lives. They have no clarity. No vision. No perspective. I find it very dispiriting I have to say.

I hate students.

**Jade**  Do you?

**Danny**  I *fucking* hate sixth-formers. All fucking iPods and crappy T-shirts with band names on.

Do you like the sea, Jade, do yer?

**Jade**  Yeah.

**Danny**  Have you ever been out past Southend before?

**Jade**  No.

**Danny**  Foulness Island. What a funny name! How old are you Jade?

**Jade**  I'm sixteen.

**Danny**  That's not what Paul told me. He told me you were fourteen. Are you fourteen or sixteen?

**Jade**  Sixteen.

**Danny**  Are you lying to try to impress me?

**Jade**  No.

**Danny**  Have you ever actually had sex before?

**Jade**  What?

**Danny**  You could look all right, you, you know? If you sorted yourself out a bit, I think you could. Sort your hair out. Your hair looks shit. There could be something of the Britney Spears about you. Do you like her? Britney? Do you, Jade? Stop crying. Jade, do you like Britney Spears?

Will you sing one of her songs for me? Jade? Have you got a good singing voice? Come on, Jade. Sing that, do you know that, that one with the school uniform on, that one 'Baby One More Time'?

Do you know that one, Jade?

Come on. You know it. Britney Spears, Jade.

*He sings the first line of the song, encouraging her to sing along with him. He does a little dance while he's singing.*

*He forgets the words, hums them. Can't stop himself laughing while he's singing.*

*He remembers the chorus. Sings it. At his manic encouragement she begins to join in.*

*He stops singing before the final line of the chorus. Waits for her to finish the line. Leans right in on her. Big grin on his face. She sings the final line of the chorus alone.*

*He nearly hits her. Hard. On the side of her head. Stops his fist just in time. Bursts out laughing.*

Do you want to travel, Jade, do you think?

**Jade**   What are you going to do to me, please?

**Danny**   Where do you want to go? Tell me somewhere. Tell me where you wanna go. Tell me some places.

**Jade**   –

**Danny**   Do you want to do a geography quiz?

**Jade**   –

**Danny**   Capital cities! Ask me a capital cities question, Jade. Go on. Ask me, 'What's the capital of . . . ?', Jade. You ask me. 'What's the capital of . . . ?' Go on, Jade.

**Jade**   I don't know.

**Danny**   You say, 'What's the capital of . . . ?' Say that, Jade! Say it! Please!

**Jade**   What's the capital of . . . ?

**Danny**   And then you think of a country. Say it again, Jade, and think of a country.

**Jade**   What's the capital of . . . ?

**Danny**   Go on, Jade.

**Jade**   Bulgaria?

**Danny**   Sofia! See! Sofia! How fucking brilliant is that?! How many men could do that, Jade?! Not fucking many, that's how many! Not. Fucking. Many!

Do you know how many words I can spell? Do you? Jade? Thousands of words. I can spell thousands of words, Jade. More than anybody I know.

Do you know how many press-ups I can do? Jade, look at me. I can do a hundred press-ups.

Here. Feel my muscles, Jade. Feel them.

*He flexes his bicep. She refuses to move her arm to touch it.*

FEEL MY MUSCLES, JADE!

*She does.*

They're hard, aren't they? Aren't my muscles hard, Jade?

**Jade**   Yes.

**Danny**   I know. Here. Watch this!

*He falls to the floor and does ten one-armed press-ups. Counts them all as he does them.*

Isn't that great?! Not many people can do that, Jade. Not many people can.

*She barely dares look at him.*

I like your jacket.

**Jade**   Thank you.

**Danny**   Is it new?

**Jade**   No.

**Danny**   It looks it.

**Jade**   It isn't.

**Danny**   It looks all shiny. Clothes are funny when they feel all new, aren't they? When they smell new. It's a good feeling, that, I think.

Take it off.

**Jade**   What?

**Danny**   I wanna take a photograph of you. On my phone.

Would you mind if I took a photograph of you, Jade? Here. Take your, your, take your jacket off, will ya? That's better. There. That's lovely. Gissa smile. Lovely.

*He pulls a mobile phone out of his pocket and takes a photograph of her.*

Do you want a Coca-Cola? Do you? You want some Coke? I've got some Coca-Cola in the car. Or how about a smoothie? Do you want a yogurt and honey smoothie? I love yogurt and honey smoothies, me.

Put your hand down. On the ground.

**Jade**   –

**Danny**   Put it there.

**Jade**   Don't.

**Danny**   Jade. Now.

*She puts one hand on the ground. He takes another photograph.*

Now keep it there.

**Jade**   –

**Danny**   I'm going to go and get some Coca-Cola and a yogurt and honey smoothie from the car. I'm not going to tell you when I'm coming back. But when I come back I want your hand to be there.

**Jade**   Please don't.

**Danny**   *smiles at her briefly, then leaves. She keeps her hand on the ground.*

*He comes back in with a bottle of Coca-Cola, a small yogurt and honey smoothie, a canister of petrol, a body bag folded up, a cushion and a cigarette in his mouth.*

*He lights the cigarette. He smokes it for a while, watching her. He puts the cigarette out on her hand. She screams. Starts crying.*

**Danny**    Did I say that you could move your hand?

**Jade**    No.

**Danny**    No, I didn't. I didn't tell you you could move your hand. So why – Jade, Jade, look at me – why did you move your hand, Jade?

**Jade**    Because you burnt me.

**Danny** *bursts into a giggle. Then stops. Gathers himself. Takes another photograph with his phone. Looks at her for a while.*

**Danny**    Here. Take your shoes off. Take your socks off.

We had. There was. Our sergeant major. He was a funny man. I quite liked him, as it goes. You hear all these stories, don't you? Attention! But, no, he was all right. He'd get drunk. Do this to you.

*He hits the soles of her feet with the butt of his gun.*

With a hammer. Never did it to me. Hurts, doesn't it? And when he shouts at you. SIT FUCKING STILL, JADE! The feeling of spittle on yer face. Here. I'll wipe it off.

*He wipes her face.*

And you can't tell anybody. You can't pull rank. You can't do that. Get a bucket of shit and piss from the slops of the drains there. Get some little geek cunt. Pour it over their head. It was quite funny. And out there. Everybody says about the British. How fucking noble we are. I used to like the Yanks. At least they were honest about it. At least they had a sense of humour. Yer get me?

*He imitates the famous Lynndie England 'Thumbs up!' sign right in her face. And puts on an American accent.*

Thumbs up, Mac!

Some of the things we did, down in Basra. It was a laugh. I'll tell yer that for nothing. Here, Ali Baba. Get that down yer throat, yer raghead cunt.

You never know. Fucking fourteen-year-old girl? Don't matter. Could've strapped herself. Underneath her fucking burka. Take it off!

**Jade**   What?

**Danny**   Take it off! Take your burka off, this is a body search. I've seen boys with their faces blown off. Skin all pussed up and melted. Eyeballs hanging out on the cartilage.

Yer helmet holds it all together. Bits of yer skull held in.

Will you pretend you're my sister? Jade?

**Jade**   –

**Danny**   Will you, Jade?

**Jade**   If you want.

**Danny**   Thanks.

*Takes another photograph with his phone.*

**Jade**   It's muscle.

**Danny**   What?

**Jade**   It's muscle, not cartilage – that holds the eyeball into the skull.

*He looks at her for a bit.*

**Danny**   Yeah.

*Looks at her for a bit more.*

Course you come back. Go up London. Fucking burkas all over the place.

*He picks up the petrol canister.*

Now here's a question for you. Is this really petrol or is it water?

*He opens the canister. Holds it open, under her nose, for her to sniff.*

What do you think? Jade? What do you think? Answer me.

**Jade**   I don't know.

**Danny**   No, I know. But have a guess. What do you reckon?

**Jade**   I think it's petrol.

**Danny**   Do yer?

**Jade**   It smells like petrol.

**Danny**   Are you sure that's not just your imagination?

**Jade**   No. I don't know.

**Danny**   Your imagination plays terrible fucking tricks on you in situations like this.

*He pours some over her head.*

You look quite funny. Your hair's all wet.

*Takes another photograph with his phone.*

You want a cigarette?

*He pulls a cigarette out of his packet. Offers it to her. She doesn't take it. He pops it in his mouth. Crouches down. Pulls out a box of matches.*

**Jade**   No.

**Danny**   Should we?

**Jade**   No, please, no, don't, don't, don't, don't. Please.

**Danny**   Chicken. Coward.

*He pulls out his gun and presses it into the cushion against her chest. He shoots her in the chest four times. There is no scream. Not much*

*blood is apparent at first. Just four dull thuds. She slumps over a bit.*
*He takes another photograph with his phone.*

*He drags her body towards the body bag, leaving a massive trail of*
*blood behind her. The shots have blown her back off. Puts her into the*
*body bag. Zips it up. He talks to her while he's working.*

Yer see them, don't yer?

Fucking leave university and get a fucking house together
and spend all day in their shitehawk little jobs hoping that
one day they're gonna make it as a fucking big shot. But
they're not. They never will. They're shrivelled up Home
Counties kids and they march against the war and think
they're being radical. They're lying. They're monkeys.
They're French exchange students. They're Australians in
London wrecked on cheap wine and shite beer. They're
Hasidic Jews in swimming pools. They're lesbian cripples
with bus passes. They're niggers, with their faces all full of
their mama's jerk chicken, shooting each other in the back
down Brixton high street until the lot of them have
disappeared. They're little dickless Paki boys training to be
doctors or to run corner shops and smuggling explosives in
rucksacks onto the top decks of buses. It's not funny, Jade.
I'm not joking. I fought a war for this lot.

I want to get it right. That isn't the right word. What's the
right word? I want to get the right word. Don't tell me.
Don't tell me. Don't tell me. I want to get it right.

I need a massage.

I can't even see straight.

Have I got a stammer? Have you noticed that?

# Seven

**Danny** *and* **Justin** *and* **Helen**.

**Danny**    Do you know any good dentists?

**Justin**    I'm sorry?

**Danny**    I was just wondering if you knew any good dentists. I've got the most fucking horrible toothache.

**Justin**    Not round here.

**Helen**    We're not actually from round here.

**Justin**    I've a good dentist in Chalk Farm, but that's no use.

**Danny**    No.

**Justin**    I'm sorry.

**Danny**    That's OK.

**Helen**    Toothache's dreadful.

**Danny**    Yeah. I fucking hate the dentist and all. It's terrifying. The sound of the drill and that.

Is that where you live? Chalk Farm?

**Helen**    It is, yes.

**Danny**    Whereabouts?

**Helen**    Do you know Chalk Farm?

**Danny**    A little, yeah.

**Helen**    Fitzjohn's Avenue. Just west of Rosslyn Hill. Do you know that bit?

**Danny**    No. I don't. I've no idea.

**Helen**    It's lovely.

**Danny**    Is it very expensive?

**Helen**    It is, yes.

**Danny**   Great!

**Helen**   I'm Helen.

**Danny**   Hi, Helen. I'm Danny.

**Helen**   Hello, Danny. How lovely to meet you.

**Danny**   And you, yeah.

**Justin**   I'm Justin.

**Danny**   Nice one. Arright, Justin?

**Justin**   Hello, mate.

**Danny**   What brings you down here then?

**Justin**   We often come to the Northview.

**Danny**   Oh yeah?

**Justin**   It's our favourite hotel.

**Danny**   Right.

**Helen**   For a day out. A night off. A night out.

**Danny**   Great.

**Helen**   We just get in the car. Book a room. Spend the night.

**Danny**   Lovely.

**Helen**   I love the sea.

**Danny**   Yeah, me too.

**Helen**   The pier. And the funfair.

**Danny**   Do yer?

**Helen**   It's marvellous.

**Danny**   That's funny to me, that.

**Helen**   Why?

**Danny**   You just don't strike me as the funfair type.

**Helen**    Don't I?

**Danny**    No.

**Justin**    Doesn't she?

**Danny**    No.

**Helen**    Well, I am.

**Justin**    She is.

**Helen**    What kind of type do I strike you as, Danny?

**Danny**    I have no fucking idea.

**Justin**    Whereabouts are you from Danny?

**Danny**    I'm from Dagenham.

**Justin**    Marvellous.

**Danny**    In Essex.

**Justin**    Yes. I know it. Up the A13.

**Danny**    That's right.

**Justin**    The Ford Factory.

**Danny**    Uh-huh.

**Justin**    The World of Leather!

**Danny**    I'm sorry?

**Justin**    There's a massive World of Leather in Dagenham. You can get leather sofas there.

**Danny**    I never knew that.

**Justin**    It's a marvellous place. Would you like a drink?

**Danny**    I'm – I don't know.

**Justin**    We're having a drink.

**Helen**    Join us.

**Justin**    Come on, mate, join us for a drink.

**Danny**  I don't know if I should. I'm driving. I've got a delivery in the boot. I've not eaten – it'd go right to my head.

**Justin**  We're just about to eat ourselves.

**Helen**  Yes. Would you like something to eat?

**Danny**  I don't have –

**Helen**  Maybe we could buy you a meal or something?

**Danny**  Thank you. I'll – I'll have a beer with you.

**Helen**  We'll see about the meal.

**Danny**  Yeah.

**Justin**  Yes.

**Helen**  Good. Lovely.

**Justin**  What are you delivering?

**Danny**  I'm sorry?

**Justin**  In your boot, what is it that you're delivering?

**Danny**  Fireworks.

**Justin**  Fireworks?!

**Helen**  How exciting!

**Danny**  Is it?

**Justin**  Why on earth have you got a delivery of fireworks in the boot of your car?

**Danny**  I arrange firework displays.

**Justin**  Do you?

**Danny**  You know, for football matches. Things like that.

**Helen**  Terrific.

**Danny**  When West Ham got promoted. I did that.

**Helen**  Isn't that marvellous?

**Justin**    Trevor Brooking!

**Danny**    Yeah.

**Justin**    What beer would you like?

**Danny**    Er . . .

**Justin**    They have a fantastic selection of multinational lagers.

**Danny**    A lager's fine. A pint of lager would be smashing. Thanks, Justin.

**Justin** *leaves.* **Helen** *crosses her legs. Stares at* **Danny**. **Danny** *feels his tooth. A time.*

**Helen**    You're rather gorgeous, aren't you?

**Danny**    I'm sorry?

**Helen**    Don't apologise. (*Beat.*) Do you work out?

**Danny**    Do I? No. No. No, I don't.

**Helen**    You've got very broad shoulders.

**Danny**    I used to be a soldier.

**Helen**    Did you?

**Danny**    Until a year or so ago.

**Helen**    I see.

**Danny**    I was out in Basra, as it goes. When that all kicked off.

**Helen**    Good God.

**Danny**    Yeah.

**Helen**    That must have been awful.

**Danny**    No. No. No. No. It was all right. It was fine.

**Helen**    Are you married, Danny?

**Danny**    I am, yeah.

**Helen**   What's your wife called?

**Danny**   Marley.

**Helen**   What a lovely name! How long have you been married to Marley, Danny?

**Danny**   Ten years. We were at school together. We got married just after we left sixth form.

**Helen**   How lovely.

**Danny**   Yeah.

**Helen**   Where's Marley now?

**Danny**   She's at home.

**Helen**   Is she expecting you back?

**Danny**   She is, yeah.

**Helen**   I see.

**Justin** *returns with a pint of lager.*

**Danny**   Thanks, Justin.

**Justin**   That's my pleasure.

**Danny**   You not having one?

**Justin**   No, no. We're all right.

**Helen**   We're fine.

*A pause.* **Danny** *drinks a big gulp of lager.*

**Helen**   A hard day?

**Danny**   Yeah. It was a bit, as it goes.

That tastes lovely.

What do you do, Justin?

**Justin**   I'm a schoolteacher.

**Danny**   Are you?

**Justin**   I am, yes. Well. I'm the head of year. At a
grammar school. In Tottenham.

**Danny**   I always hated schoolteachers.

**Justin**   Is that right?

**Danny**   Well. I say that. It's actually a lie. They always
used to hate me. I would often hanker after their affections.
Never got it. It was a big disappointment to me.

**Justin**   I can imagine.

**Danny**   Do you work?

**Helen**   I do, yes.

**Danny**   What do you do?

**Helen**   I manage a television production company.

**Danny**   That sounds pretty, er, exhausting.

**Helen**   It is.

**Danny**   Does it affect you at all?

**Helen**   How do you mean?

**Danny**   My dad was in management. It gave him a
certain demeanour. I think it affected his posture a bit. He
used to stand up incredibly straight.

**Helen**   I'm not sure. I've never thought about it. You have
a look. Let me know.

*She stands to leave. Speaks to* **Justin** *first.*

**Helen**   I think so, don't you?

**Justin** *smiles. The two men watch her leave.* **Danny** *drinks.*

*Some time passes.*

**Danny**   Thank you for the beer. It's lovely. Really hits the
spot.

**Justin**   That's my pleasure. Honestly.

*Pause.*

**Danny**    Yeah.

*Some time.*

**Justin**    So. Fireworks.

**Danny**    That's right.

*Some time passses.* **Justin** *looks right at him.*

**Justin**    Helen's my wife.

**Danny**    I guessed that.

**Justin**    We've actually got two children.

**Danny**    Oh, right.

**Justin**    David is four and Phillipa's two.

**Danny**    Lovely.

**Justin**    They're staying with her mother tonight.

**Danny**    Right.

**Justin**    Have you been to this hotel before?

**Danny**    I haven't, no.

**Justin**    I didn't think you had.

**Danny**    It's all right, isn't it? The views and that.

**Justin**    It is. Yes. We're staying in Room 21.

**Danny**    I'm sorry?

**Justin**    Room 21.

*Some time passes.*

**Danny** *breaks into a big grin.* **Justin** *smiles with him.*

**Danny**    Fucking hell.

**Justin**    Don't say anything now.

*Some time.*

**Helen** *comes back. They sit together for a bit.* **Justin** *and* **Helen** *exchange glances, slight smiles, while* **Danny** *drinks more of his beer.*

**Danny**   Justin was just telling me about your children.

**Helen**   What did he say about them?

**Danny**   He told me how old they were.

**Helen**   Did he? Did you?

**Justin**   I did.

**Danny**   Four and two, wasn't it? David and Phillipa?

**Helen**   That's right.

**Justin**   Pip, I call her.

**Helen**   He's completely devoted to her. Aren't you?

**Justin**   I am a bit, I'm afraid.

**Helen**   He's absolutely under her thumb. She's got him twisted round her little finger.

**Danny**   He invited me up to your room.

**Helen**   Did he?

**Danny**   I'm a bit fucking freaked out, as it goes.

**Helen**   I thought you would be. There's no need to be.

Danny was telling me, Justin, while you were at the bar. He used to be in the army.

**Justin**   You can tell that.

**Helen**   That's what I thought. He was in Basra, apparently.

**Justin**   Were you really?

**Danny** *chuckles a bit.*

**Justin**   Would you like another beer?

**Danny**   No, thank you. I'm all right.

**Justin**   It's not a big deal, you know? It's just an invitation. I think Helen finds you quite attractive. But you mustn't do anything that you don't want to do.

**Danny**   No. No. No. It's not that. It's just a surprise.

**Helen**   It's just sex.

**Danny**   Yeah. I think it's good. My mum never bothered asking my dad. I think it's very open-minded. Does that come with working in the media, do you think?

**Helen**   I'm not entirely sure.

**Danny**   And do you like to watch, do you?

**Justin**   Only if it's not a problem.

**Danny**   Or do you join in?

**Justin**   I think that's . . .

**Helen**   That can be up to you.

**Danny**   Right.

**Helen** *stands up.*

**Helen**   I think you two should decide that. I'll be back.

*She leaves.*

**Danny**   I guess it's one of those things, isn't it? That you read about.

**Justin**   I don't know, is it?

**Danny**   It goes on all the time, I bet.

**Justin** *nods.*

**Danny**   Do you like it? Watching?

**Justin**   I do, yes.

**Danny**   Why?

**Justin**   I think it's lovely. I like to watch her happy.

**Danny**    Right. That's quite sweet, as it goes.

**Justin** *smiles.*

**Danny**    It's not like it's the first time I've ever come across this kind of thing, you know.

**Justin**    No?

**Danny**    In our platoon. You could go, sometimes, into downtown Basra.

**Justin**    Really?

**Danny**    Or not even bother. You could just stay in the barracks. Fuck each other. That would happen. You can't blame people, can you?

**Justin**    I never would.

**Danny**    You do get a little bored after a while.

**Justin**    I can imagine.

**Danny**    Smell of a nice bit of aftershave. Nice bit of stubble on a chin. All the same with your eyes closed, isn't it? There is a certain attraction, I think.

**Justin**    I think so, too.

**Danny**    I thought you would. I was lying. Yer gay cunt.

**Justin**    I don't believe you.

**Danny**    You what?

**Justin**    I don't believe you were lying.

**Helen** *comes back. There is a time. She stares at him. Grins.*

**Helen**    You're still here. I'm glad. (*To* **Justin**.) Thank you.

**Justin** *smiles at* **Danny**.

**Danny**    Did you go on the march?

**Justin**    On the –

**Danny**   On the anti-war march, up Hyde Park, did you two go on that?

**Justin**   Yes. We did.

**Danny** *laughs.*

**Danny**   Did yer?!

**Helen**   Why's that funny?

**Danny**   I wish I'd been there.

**Justin**   Do you?

**Danny**   With my SA80. Sprayed the lot of yer. Stick that up yer arse and smoke it, Damon Albarn, yer fucking pikey cunt.

**Helen** *and* **Justin** *smile at one another.*

**Helen**   Yes.

**Danny**   I come back home. It's a completely foreign country.

*He reaches over to* **Helen**. *Strokes her cheek.*

**Danny**   'Do you work out?' What the fuck are you talking about? Two hours' drill and forty lengths. Twenty-five minutes max. Alternate strokes. Breaststroke, front crawl, backstroke, butterfly.

*He puts his thumb in her mouth. She sucks on it.*

Here, you'll like this. I saw, onc time, a group of guys, at Pirbright, get another lad, a younger lad – no, listen to this, this is right up your street. They get him. Hold him down. Get a broom handle. Fucking push it, right up his rectum. Right up there. (*He removes his thumb.*) And we all watched that. Joined in. That was funny, to be fair. It did feel funny. I imagine it's the same kind of feeling, is it?

**Helen**   Are you trying to unnerve us?

**Danny**    Mind you, you play that game out there and it's even funnier. 'Cause they don't like anything with the slightest sexual connotation. You two, out there! Fucking hell!

**Justin** (*smiling*)    I think he is.

**Helen**    Do you?

**Danny**    I'd put it on my phone. You wanna see what I've got on my phone? You wanna see Ken Bigley? I've got Ken Bigley on here. Nick Berg. All them! You wanna watch?

**Justin**    I think you are.

**Danny**    You wanna watch, Justin?

**Justin**    No, I don't.

**Danny** *stares at him.*

**Danny**    Do you know what I want to do?

**Helen**    What's that?

**Danny**    I want an arm-wrestle. Right now. I fucking love arm-wrestles, me. Do you want one, Justin?

**Helen**    You're rather funny, aren't you?

**Justin** (*chuckling*)    He's like a little boy.

**Danny**    Justin. Come here. Let's have an arm-wrestle.

*He positions his arm. Glares at him.*

Come on, mate.

**Justin** *braces* **Danny**'s *arm in an arm-wrestle.* **Danny** *holds his arm exactly where he wants it.*

**Danny**    I've put children into the backs of ambulances and they've not *got* any arms, actually.

It could happen here, all that. I reckon it will. There are too many people. Wait until the water runs out. And the oxygen runs out.

**Justin**   Are you trying your hardest?

**Danny**   I'm gonna convert to Islam. Save me from scumballs like you two.

I'm not apologising for anything. See me. I'm as innocent as a baby. I'm a fucking hero! I'm a fucking action hero. I'm John fucking Wayne! I'm Sylvester Stallone! I'm fucking James Bond, me!

*He wins the arm-wrestle.*

That was fucking easy.

## Eight

**Danny** *and* **Lee**.

**Lee**   I spoke to Mum.

**Danny**   Right.

**Lee**   I told them to tell anybody who asks that you were with them all day.

**Danny**   Right.

**Lee**   She said she would. She said that Dad would too. She said it's not a problem. They've not been out. They've not spoken to anybody.

**Danny**   Which is lucky.

**Lee**   Yes. Yes. Yes. Yes. It is. Yes. They won't ask.

**Danny**   What?

**Lee**   Mum and Dad. They won't ask why they've got to lie for you.

**Danny**   No.

**Lee**   They'll just do it. They'll do whatever I ask them to.

**Danny**   Right. Yeah. Course they will. What'll you say?

**Lee**    I, I, I, I, I, I, I, I –

*They look at each other for a long time.*

**Danny**    I've had one hell of a day.

*They look at each other for a long time.*

It's horrible round here. They should set it on fire.

*They look at each other for a long time.*

Don't tell anybody, Lee. Don't you dare. Do you
understand me?

**Lee**    Of course I do.

**Danny**    You fucking better.

**Lee**    What are you going to do?

**Danny**    When?

**Lee**    If the police find you?

**Danny**    I'll shoot them in the face and then shoot myself
in the face and all.

**Lee**    I'm being serious.

**Danny**    So am I, Lee.

*Pause.*

**Lee**    Can I see it?

**Danny**    See what?

**Lee**    Your gun.

**Danny** *gets his gun out of his pocket and shows it to* **Lee**. **Lee**
*holds it with a mix of complete horror and absolute fascination.*

**Danny**    It's hot, isn't it? We should go out. Take our shoes
off. Get the grass between our toes.

So.

Blackburn next week, Lee.

**Lee** (*completely transfixed by the gun*)   That's right. Mark Hughes was a good player. Sparky, they called him.

**Danny**   Are you going to go, do you think?

**Lee**   I don't think so, no.

**Danny**   Have you ever actually been? To a game?

**Lee**   No. I haven't, no.

**Danny**   Why not?

**Lee**   I don't know. I haven't.

**Danny**   I wish I had a sister. It would have been miles better.

**Lee**   How much money have you got, exactly?

**Danny**   Three thousand, two hundred pounds.

**Lee**   Right. That's one good thing. (*Beat.*) Where is she, Danny?

**Danny**   She's in the boot of the car.

**Lee**   What are you gonna do with her?

**Danny**   I have no idea.

**Lee** *gives the gun back.*

**Lee**   Have my fingerprints all over that now. They'll think I did it.

**Danny**   Nobody'll notice that she's gone, you know?

**Lee**   They will. She was fourteen.

**Danny**   You didn't know her. She wasn't like most fourteen-year-olds.

**Lee**   This is stupid. You're stupid. You're a stupid stupid stupid stupid stupid –

**Danny**   What?

I wish it hadn't happened, Lee.

**Lee**   Do you?

**Danny**   If that's any consolation.

**Lee**   It isn't.

**Danny**   She was like a doll. She was a cute little black thing.

How was your lunch?

**Lee**   It was very nice, thank you.

**Danny**   What did you have?

**Lee**   I had roast pork and apple sauce and roast potatoes and gravy and carrots and peas and cauliflower.

**Danny**   You wouldn't get that free if you were living with Mum and Dad, would you? Doctors wouldn't come round then, would they?

**Lee**   I don't think so.

**Danny**   Is that the main reason you left, Lee, for yer dinners? Do you really think you deserve this place?

**Lee**   I don't know.

**Danny**   Is that why you keep it so fucking clean?

**Lee**   Danny.

**Danny**   Do you think it's Mum and Dad's fault, what's happening to you? Is it genetic, do you think?

**Lee**   Don't you start swearing your head off again!

**Danny**   Did you have a hundred fucking mercury fillings or what?

**Lee**   Danny.

**Danny**   You don't have the slightest idea what I'm going through.

**Lee**   Did you go and see Marley?

*Pause.*

**Danny**    I did, yeah.

**Lee**    I told you not to go.

**Danny**    I know.

**Lee**    You liked her, didn't you?

**Danny**    I did, yeah.

**Lee**    You liked her a bit too much, I think. You would've married her, I bet.

**Danny**    Lee.

**Lee**    She would never have married you, would she though, Danny? You were completely deluding yourself.

I'm so much cleverer than you, in real life, it's embarrassing.

When you were on television. I was incredulous. You couldn't even finish your sentences.

Thing is. Mum and Dad were extremely proud of you. They had arguments. Over which one of them you took after and which one I took after.

He's ashamed of me, Dad. Which is ironic. And if it weren't for you, I would have had a much more horrible time than I actually did. People were frightened you would have battered them. On account of you being a psychopath. I know that. But I can't do this, I don't think.

**Danny**    Do what?

**Lee**    Your eyes.

**Danny**    What can't you do, Lee?

**Lee**    I'm not surprised that girls like you. You've got nice eyes. They look for nice eyes in a man, I heard.

**Danny**    Lee, I asked you a question.

**Lee**    I don't think I can not tell. I think I'm going to tell the police.

**Danny**    Lee.

**Lee**   I don't think I can keep it to myself.

**Danny**   You can, you can, you can, you can, Lee.

**Lee**   Are you gonna batter my head in now?

**Danny**   You so can. You so can.

**Lee**   Why should I?

**Danny**   You're my brother.

*They look at each other for a long time. The longest that they can manage. And then* **Danny** *moves away.*

Ah, fuck it! Eh? Eh, Lee? Fuck it! You know?

It doesn't matter.

What does it matter?

Here. Bruv. Come here. I'm sorry I was mean to you! I think you're the best. I think you're fucking gorgeous. Come here.

**Lee** *approaches him.*

**Danny**   Touch my chest.

**Lee** *rests his hand on his chest.*

**Danny**   There. How hard is that? You like that? Here. Come here.

*He beckons* **Lee** *towards his face.*

**Danny**   Come on. Just a kiss. There.

*He kisses* **Lee**, *on the lips.*

**Danny**   There. You don't need to tell anybody. Do you?

Have you got a hard-on? You have, haven't you? It's all right. It's all right, Lee. Straight up. It's all right. It doesn't matter.

All our years. All of them.

My brother!

He knows what I'm talking about.

When we were kids. Tell yer.

And everybody looks at him like he's some kind of fucked-up fucking weird old cunt. But he's not, yer know.

He's not.

He isn't.

He's all right.

He's not gonna tell anybody.

And the way you smell! It's exactly the way I smell too. It reminds me of me. It makes me feel sick.

*He kisses* **Lee** *hard on the cheek. And breaks away. Lights a cigarette. His hands trembling.*

**Lee**   You smoke the same brand as Dad's secret cigarettes.

**Danny**   Right.

**Lee**   It must be genetic.

*Pause.*

**Danny**   Will you cut my hair?

**Lee**   What?

**Danny**   I need a haircut.

**Lee**   All right.

**Danny**   I've got clippers.

**Lee**   I don't need your clippers. I've got my own clippers. I'll do it with my clippers. I'll do it great.

*He pulls up a chair.* **Danny** *sits in it.* **Lee** *wraps a towel round* **Danny***'s neck. Leaves to go and get his clippers.*

**Danny** *stares out.*

**Lee** *comes back after a bit.*

**Danny**   Shanghai.

**Lee**   12,762,953.

**Danny**   Moscow.

**Lee**   10,381,288.

*He stands behind* **Danny**, *looks at the back of his head. He has the clippers poised in his hand.*

**Danny**   In Basra, when it all kicked off with the prisoners, I didn't do any of it. I never touched nobody. I had the rules, pinned above my head. My idiot's guide to the Geneva Convention pinned to the head of my bed. They used to call me a pussy cunt. It never used to bother me. I wish I'd told somebody. I might, still. I wish I'd joined in. I would've liked that.

I don't blame the war.

The war was all right. I miss it.

It's just you come back to this.

**Lee**   I never touched *any*body.

**Danny**   You what?

**Lee**   It's I never touched *any*body. Not I never touched *no*body. That's just careless.

**Lee** *turns his clippers on. He waits for a while before he starts cutting.*

*The lights fall.*

# Pornography

*Pornography* was originally translated into German by Barbara Christ and was first presented in a co-production between the Deutsches Schauspielhaus, Hamburg, and the Festival Theaterformen and the Schauspielhannover in Hanover. It received its world premiere in Hanover on 15 June 2007 and transferred to Hamburg on 5 October 2007. The cast was as follows:

Sonja Beisswenger
Christoph Franken
Peter Knaack
Angela Muethel
Jana Schulz
Monique Schwitter
Daniel Wahl
Samuel Weiss

*Director* Sebastian Nübling
*Designer* Muriel Gerstner
*Lighting* Roland Edrich
*Music* Lars Wittershagen
*Costume designer* Marion Münch
*Dramaturgs* Nicola Bramkamp, Regina Guhl, David Tushingham

*Pornography* received its British premiere at the Traverse Theatre, Edinburgh, on 28 July 2008. The cast was as follows:

Frances Ashman
Loo Brealey
Sacha Dhawan
Amanda Hale
Jeff Rawle
Sheila Reid
Billy Seymour
Sam Spruell

| | |
|---|---|
| *Director* | Sean Holmes |
| *Designer* | Paul Wills |
| *Lighting* | Chris Davey |
| *Sound* | Emma Laxton |

This play can be performed by any number of actors.
It can be performed in any order.

I am going to keep this short and to the point, because it's all been said before by far more eloquent people than me.

But our words have no impact upon you, therefore I'm going to talk to you in a language that you understand. Our words are dead until we give them life with our blood.

*Images of hell.*
*They are silent.*

What you need to do is stand well clear of the yellow line.

*Images of hell.*
*They are silent.*

## Seven

I wake up and I think he's drowning. I can hear the sound of him in his cot. His breath is tight and he's gasping. I go into his room. Stand there. Every bone is as small as a finger. He's not drowning. Of course he's not drowning, he's on dry land. It's Saturday morning. He's still asleep. I watch his chest rise and fall. It would take only the lightest of forces from an adult's arm to crush the bones in his ribcage. I feel so much love for him that my heart fills up. I can feel it filling up. Like a balloon.

It's six thirty.

I go back into my bedroom. I crawl under the covers. Jonathan, my husband, is lying on his side. When I get back into the bed he lays his arm across me. It's incredibly heavy. Like it's made out of leather.

I wait for Lenny, for my son, to wake up.

He does.

I turn the radio on downstairs. I put the kettle on. I put Lenny in his chair. He's grumpy this morning. I make a pot

of three cups of Jamaican Blue Mountain coffee. And
slowly, methodically, I sit and drink all three cups myself.

I let Jonathan sleep.

I don't remember any news story that was on the radio that
day. Apart from everybody's talking about, there's a
concert. A man's talking about this concert. And exactly
what it is going to achieve I must admit I find a little
unclear. But he's deeply passionate about the whole affair.
And the singer's passion, and Lenny's grumpiness, the little
tiny whining noises that he makes, and the taste of the coffee
and the feeling of wood on my table means that I find, to
my surprise, that there are tears pouring down my face and
falling onto the newspaper which the boy, some boy, a boy I
think, at least I think it's a boy, delivered, must have
delivered at some point this morning.

I go shopping in the afternoon and in my head I'm already
getting prepared for work next week.

I push Lenny in his pushchair. He's got one of those three-
wheeled pushchairs. It has fabulous suspension. It makes it
ideal for city street life. I buy myself a pair of sandals which
are pink and they have this golden strap with a little pink
flower on. I think in the shops everybody's got the concert
on. It's that man I like. He's singing the song about looking
at the stars. Look at the stars. See how they shine for you.
Maybe today is the most important day that there's ever
been. And this is the biggest success of human organisation
that we've ever known. And everybody should be given a
knighthood of some description. There should be some kind
of knighthood which is given out to all of the people there.
To the people who sell the ice creams even. They should get
an ice-cream seller's knighthood. For the important selling
of ice cream at a time of organisational urgency. I'd like to
watch the Queen knight the boys selling ice cream in Hyde
Park today. She wouldn't even need to walk far from her
house. She could go on a bike. It would take her five minutes.
This is a day of that level of importance.

I'm pushing him so much that he falls to sleep in the end.
You bump up and down. I want to walk home. I could duck
south of Euston Road. I could head through Bloomsbury.
Today is a day for heading through Bloomsbury with a new
pair of summer sandals, ideal for the beach, on a Saturday.

I don't.

I start off.

And then I get the bus from Holborn.

And I get home and Jonathan's not there. He should be
there. He should be at home. I don't have the slightest idea
where he is. I try not to think about it. The house is quieter
without him.

Where were you? Where were you? Which shops? What
were you doing? What were you doing there? What were
you buying? What are you going to paint? I want to know
what you need paint for. I want to know what you want to
paint. I want to know where you've been. Do you like my
sandals? I bought some sandals, do you like them? I bought
them for the beach. For the summer.

Sunday's Jonathan's day with Lenny. He takes him to buy
newspapers. I sleep in. But Lenny starts crying when
Jonathan's putting his shoes on. He's putting his shoes on
wrong. His socks are bunched up over his feet. He's put his
little socks on and not pulled them up properly and they're
all bunched up so the shoes are uncomfortable and he starts
to cry. I say to myself I am not getting up out of bed to help
him. I am not getting up out of bed to help him. I am not
getting up out of bed to help him.

They leave. I have no idea what I'm going to do today. I sit
still for up to half an hour at a time.

I don't know where he takes him. He's windswept when he
comes back. Windswept and scruffy and Lenny's crabby but
happy. When Jonathan's hair is like that. When his hair is
all over the place and there's a sense that he's been outside

because his cheeks are all pink. I look at him and there's something about him which is enough to make me smile.

We eat our tea in front of the television when Lenny's in bed. I want Jonathan to touch me. If he were to reach out and touch me. Just rest his hand on my neck and stroke the back of my hair. If he were to do that now. Right now. Right this second.

I drop Lenny off at Julia's and he squeaks with happiness.

The tube is full of people and nearly all of them nowadays have iPods. I can't remember when that happened.

I head into work.

The Triford report is nearly finished. It's nearly ready. When it's ready. If we get it right. If David gets it right then the implications for the company are, well, they are immense. We actually did have to sign a contract that forbade us to speak even to our spouses about what was going on. It's a legally binding contract. There are rumours that Catigar Jones are working in a similar area. But David thinks they're months behind our work. Their R&D is flawed. R&D is the key to these things. David doesn't smile at me. He doesn't wish me good morning. He doesn't ask about Lenny. Or about my weekend. He asks me if I'm feeling ready. This is a big week.

I take my lunch break in Russell Square. All I ever seem to eat any more is duck hoisin wraps. I ring Julia. Lenny's fine. Everything's fine.

Jonathan doesn't ring.

At the end of the afternoon, there's a man in the square who's taken his top off and started doing press-ups. On my way back home I watch him. I watch the muscles down his spine. I watch the rivulets of sweat on the back of his neck.

At home, I am very tempted to explain to Jonathan exactly about the Triford report. To tell him in complete detail about the nature of the report. Explain it to him meticulously. Encourage him to sell the details to Catigar Jones.

He's watching the news. There's been another car bomb in a market in Baghdad. There's always a car bomb in a market in Baghdad. I don't watch. I try to read my magazine. I'd rather watch *Sex and the City*. *Sex and the City* is on. Can we watch *Sex and the City*, please?

I want to go on a long-haul flight. I'd like to take Lenny on a long-haul flight. I like the screens, the in-flight maps on the backs of the seats in front of you. They allow you to trace the arc of the flight. They allow you to see the size of the world. They allow you to imagine the various war zones that you're flying over. You're flying over war zones. You're flying over Iraq. You're flying over Iran. You're flying over Afghanistan. And Turkmenistan. And Kazakhstan. And Chechnya. On your long-haul flight. On your way out on holiday. With the sandals that you bought with the gold strap and the plastic pink flower.

When Lenny sleeps he sticks him bum in the air. He sleeps on his knees. He wraps his blanket around himself. He's incredibly sweaty. It's Monday night and I get up again and get out of bed to check he's all right. Jonathan doesn't notice I've gone. I lie down on the floor next to his cot. Watch him breathe. Fall asleep on his floor. I go back to bed at about five o'clock and can't sleep. What did he want to buy paint for? Where did he go to buy his paint?

In the morning I can't decipher all of the different news stories on the radio.

Jonathan comes downstairs in a suit and he's so clean. His hair is clean. And his skin. He's had a shave. He grabs a banana and runs out of the door.

The freezer needs defrosting. There's a crust of ice that sits on everything. It takes a while to open the drawer and chip away at the cubes. They always make the same sound when you drop them in the glass. And their frost is settled by the whisky. My hand is shaking. It's eight in the morning. It's Tuesday. It feels fucking amazing.

I manage to get a *Metro*. I enjoy the cartoons in the *Metro*. And the photographs of pop stars on marches. All of them. Hundreds of pop stars walking hundreds and hundreds of miles. All the way through the fields of East Scotland.

Politicians have immense respect for pop stars that walk hundreds and hundreds of miles through fields in East Scotland. Their eyes light up when they see one.

There are seventy-two unread messages in my inbox. Nearly all of them relate to the Triford report.

David hasn't slept, he says. He was working on a polish. On two polishes actually. He completed one polish at about eight thirty. He went out for a Chinese meal and afterwards instead of going home he came back and worked all night on another polish. That makes two polishes in one night. The polish is the key stage, he tells me. The polish and the R&D are the key stages of any report. He asks me to print off a copy of the conclusion. I print it off on the wrong type of paper. I print it off on photographic paper. There's photographic paper in the machine and I don't check and he roars at me. Don't I realise what I've done? Don't I realise how much more difficult it is to shred photographic paper? Why didn't I check? Wasn't I thinking? Don't I think? Don't I ever fucking think?

In the afternoon it's like David has been for a shower somewhere. Maybe over his lunch break he went for a swim and got himself a shower after his swim. He doesn't talk to me. I tell him I'm sorry. He says well. You know. There are some people for whom this report means something and some people for whom it clearly doesn't mean so much. He asks me what time I'm working until tonight. I tell him I'll be there until nine. Maybe ten. He doesn't think he'll make it that long. He needs to crash he says. His work is done.

He leaves at six thirty.

Jonathan's picking Lenny up from Julia's tonight because I have to stay late because of the report. I'm on my own. In the office I'm on my own. I recheck the report. I run the figures another time. I double-check the statistics. I become indescribably bored. David has a photograph of himself on his desk. This is surprising to me. I look for jokes on Yahoo. There are images of Sebastian Coe who is getting ready for the announcement in Singapore tomorrow. All of the people there will wear the same coloured jackets, it says.

I take the report from David's desk. It's nine thirty at night. It's a Tuesday night. There's nobody else in the office. Maybe there's nobody else in the whole building. Maybe tonight there's nobody else in the whole city. I turn on the photocopier. Warming Up. Please Wait. I turn each page individually face down onto the glass. I go to the fax machine. I find the number for Catigar Jones. Fax/Start. Set.

At midday the next day, I went to see what had happened. And the BBC website said London. For about three minutes I couldn't believe it. I had to check it and check it and recheck it again.

Are you laughing or crying?
What?
I said are you laughing or are you crying?

I don't go in on Thursday. They don't want me to go in on Thursday.

I was the only person in the office on Tuesday night.

I won't take Lenny to see Julia today.

I pick him up and bring him into bed with me. I tickle his tummy. I blow raspberries on his tummy. What did he need paint for? I daren't ask him where he goes for his lunch breaks. Who is he on the phone to on his lunch breaks?

I can feel his ribs underneath his tummy and he's giggling and when he giggles his legs kick up into the air.

I look into his eyes and he looks right at me. Like he knows I was the only person in the office on Tuesday night and he finds it immensely, immensely funny.

The radio's on. Somebody's calling into a phone-in show.
He's just been woken up by a friend of his phoning him
from just south of Russell Square. There's a bus in Russell
Square, he said.

*Images of hell.*
*They are silent.*

## Six

I wasn't born here. They tell me I was born here, it's not
true.

'What the fuck are you talking about, Jason, eh? What the
fuck are you like?'

I'm Italian, I'm half Italian. How can I be half Italian if I
was born around here?

My mum and dad live here. They live in this house. They've
got one room. My sister's twenty-three. She's got one room.
I've got one room.

They're completely the same to me. They have exactly the
same skin and exactly the same structure of their face. And
exactly the same hairstyles. Their clothes are exactly the
same. I can't even tell the fucking difference between them
half the time.

Dad comes home. Mum's watching the television.

What have you been doing?
You what?
While I've been at work all day. What have you been doing?
I cleaned the house.
You did what?
I cleaned the house. The house. I cleaned it.
Did you?
I did as it goes.
It doesn't fucking look fucking clean.

You what?
I said it doesn't fucking look fucking clean.

Every day.

I don't even like them.

I don't act like them.

You should have seen my sister at school. And I get there
and everybody tells me that they taught my sister.

I bet you did.
I'm sorry, Jason?
I said I bet you fucking did.

Sometimes I go into her bedroom and I lie under her bed.

One time she came in. She didn't know I was there. She
moved around. She took something from out of a drawer.
Closed the drawer. Left the room. My heart was beating so
loudly I could feel the blood pressure in my ears.

I got out from under her bed. I got to the drawer that she
opened. Ran my hand through her clothes.

I picked up a stick of lipstick. It was a dull, pink lipstick. I
lifted it to my nose. Smelt it. I opened it up. Licked it a little
bit. I put some on. I was preparing in some ways. I was
getting myself ready in a lot of ways.

The first time I saw her in school I didn't really notice her.
That's quite funny. If you were to say to me, the first time
you saw her in school you didn't notice her. Or the first time
you see her you won't notice her. I'd look at you – I'd give
you my look like –

I don't like it. The school. It's not a good school. Don't
believe anybody who tells you that as schools go it's not a
bad school. Because that's a lie. And we have enough lies in
the world, I think.

The rules here are the rules of the insane.

Don't walk on the left-hand side.
Don't chew gum.

Don't drink water in the corridor.
Don't go to the toilet.
Tuck your shirt in.
Don't stand up.
Unless in Assembly.
Then don't sit down. Ever.

The teachers stand in front of a class and they can't control
it. They stand there. Their eyes going this way and that
way. Their arms flapping about. They can't control their
eyes. They can't control their arms let alone a –

Will you be quiet please?
I asked you to be quiet.
I won't ask you again.
I'm going to count to five and if you're not quiet.
One. Two. Three. Four. Five.

On the days when she wears a grey skirt it's like everything
has come together at once. Did you ever get a day like that?

I found out that her name was Lisa. I wrote it down.

I wanted to do a BTEC in computers. I don't suppose I'll
get the chance now.

There are things wrong with this world. I think when you
look at the power that Pakistani people have. And the
money they make. There are black people up London and
they have meat cleavers. They'll properly kill you. There are
Gypsies out by Goresbrook. They take your bike. You'll be
going past them on your bike and they'll stop you and
they'll say to you – get off your bike. Give it to us. Give us
your phone. Give us your trainers. Say you have a nice pair
of trainers. Say you saved up or your mum saved up and
bought you a nice pair of trainers. They'll just take it. I
don't think that's right. Don't tell me you think that's right
because it's not.

And white people. The white people round here are left
with nothing to do. The women wear clothes that only have
one real purpose really. I am part of an Aryan race. I came

out of nowhere. It didn't used to be like this. Why do you
think it's like this now?

I ask her. Why do you think it's like this now?
She gives me a smile that I swear I've never seen before on
any other human being and she says to me, 'I have no idea,
Jason, you tell me.'

I'm going through the Heathway and I only see one of them
at first. He walks towards me.
Aright, Jason?
Pushes into me. Pushes me around.
And before I notice it there's been another one comes up
behind me.
You stood on my toe.
I didn't.
You stood on my fucking toe, you fucking retard cunt.
I didn't mean to. It was an accident. I –
Are you calling me a liar?
Are you calling him a liar, Jason?
Don't call him a liar.
There's a third.
I'd cut his face off if I was you.

I think one of them has a screwdriver.

I'm running across the Heathway into the mall there.
I don't turn round to see where they are.
There's a railing on the side of the Heathway and it slows
me down and they catch me.
And they push me to the ground.
And one of them stamps on my face. He holds my face there
with his foot.
The other has a screwdriver pressed against my cheek.
You fucking pikey thick fucking cunt. You are dead. You
call me a liar. You are so fucking dead.
Don't. Don't. Please don't. Please don't. Don't. Don't.

What happened to your face?

There's blood on my face.
On my shirt. On the pavement. I go into the toilets of the
shopping mall and wash it off.

I don't tell my mum anything.
I don't tell my dad anything.
I don't tell my sister anything.
I have my tea like nothing happened.

I used to deserve this.
I used to be really mouthy in class.
I have the capacity to be really horrible to people.
I have been really horrible to people.
I have been horrible to people about their mothers.
I'm not any more.
This kind of thing used to happen to me all the time.
I don't deserve it any more.

There are ways of smoking cigarettes that I've experimented
with. You can smoke a cigarette like this. Or you can smoke
a cigarette like this. You can light a match like this. Or like
this. Or like this. If you're smoking draw, which is another
name for marijuana, then you should probably smoke it like
this.

Lisa smokes Marlboro Lights. Which is about as fucking
obvious as you could ever get.

I go downstairs and my sister's watching Coldplay. They're
singing that song about looking at the stars. I want to kick
the television screen in. Sometimes you think about kicking
things in like that. Stomp on his teeth.

When's Snoop Dog on?
Half five.
You gonna watch him? You gonna watch him? You
watching Snoop Dog?

She says nothing. I go out.

I found Lisa's name in the phone book. I found her address
in the phone book. You wouldn't have thought it would be
so easy, would you? I go to her house. I stand outside her

house. There's nobody there. Nobody's home. Nobody comes in. Nobody goes out. There's a pub on her corner and they've got the concert on while I'm waiting.

Madonna brings this coon onstage with her.

Are you ready, London? Are you ready to start a revolution? Are you ready to change history?

I go back the next day and the house is still empty. Maybe she's gone away for the weekend. Maybe she's gone to see some relatives or something like that. I have a cigarette while I'm waiting. I keep a packet of ten cigarettes in the lining of my blazer. After a bit I go right up to her window. I wonder which of these rooms her bedroom is. I can only see the front room. I imagine her in her front room. Watching the television. With the curtain closed. I could come round. Watch the television with her.

Miss.
Yes, Jason?
How are you today?
I'm good thank you, Jason. How are you?
I'm all right. Did you watch *Live 8*?
I watched bits of it.
Did you enjoy it?
I did, yes.
Who did you enjoy best?
I don't know.
Did you like Snoop Dog?
I didn't see him.
Do you think we'll get the Olympics, Miss?
I'm not sure. I think Paris might get it.
It'd be better there, don't you think?
I don't know.
I think it would. It would be better in Paris than in London.
London stinks, I reckon. Don't you think, Miss? Don't you think London stinks? I think it does. I think it stinks. I think it stinks of dead people.

Monday night. I get home. I think Dad's started hitting
Mum. I'm not sure. There are bruises across her face. I ask
her. She tells me not to be so ridiculous.

Tuesday morning. Lisa's wearing a red blouse and a grey
skirt. Her hair has come loose at the end of the day. She
asks me if she can get past. I let her pass. She's being rude to
me. I think she's being rude to me. Why's she being rude to
me today? How come she's started being rude to me?

And later she starts talking to the head of maths. It makes
me want to cut his throat open.

Next day. Next maths lesson. This is hilarious. I won't stop
talking. He sends me out. I won't move.

You can't make me.
You can't make me move.
You can't touch me.
You touch me and I'm going to the police.
Sir, you touch me and I'm going to the police.
Sir, do you fancy Miss Watson?
Sir, do you know where she lives? She lives on Parsloes
Avenue, doesn't she? Have you been round there?

I could buy a knife. That wouldn't be difficult. I could buy a
gun. I could get really fucking drunk and get myself a gun.

How did you find out where I live? Jason, this is serious.
It's in the phone book, Miss. It's not difficult. Do you want
a cigarette?
What are you doing here?
I'm just sitting here.
Can you move please?
You were wrong about the Olympics, Miss.
I was what?
I can't fucking believe it myself. I think they must all be
insane. Did you see them? Don't you think they're insane?
Don't you think Lord Sebastian Coe is insane, Miss? And
David Beckham.
Jason, can you move away from my house please?

Where were you at the weekend, Miss?
Where, what?
Where were you at the weekend? You weren't in all
weekend. Did you go away for the weekend?
Jason, get off my wall this instant.
Or what?
If you don't get off my wall this instant then I swear I will
call the police.
Are you worried about losing your job?
Am I what?
Because teachers and students aren't really meant to fall in
love with each other. I'd look after you though. If you did.
Jason, what on earth are you talking about?

There's a fizzing sound. Sometimes with an ashtray or a
wall or something you have to rub and rub the cigarette in.
It's not like that this time.

Let me say this. Now. After everything that's happened. I
would cut out her cunt with a fork. I would scrape off her
tits. I would force a chair leg up her arse until her rectum
bled. I would do these things. If I was forced to I would do
all of these things. Don't think I wouldn't because I would.

On my way up Oxlow Lane there's this guy. He stares at me
like he's seen something in my eyes. He's drunk. I think
drunk people are the worst. I didn't know if he was going to
hit me or kick me or what. He looked at me as though he
recognised something. And then he started smiling.

I get home and I go to my room and I put a CD on. I can't
stop thinking about the way it made a fizzing sound. It
shouldn't have made a fizzing sound. That was a complete
surprise to me.

I'd like to go on a roller coaster. Right now that's what I
would like. To go to Chessington or Alton Towers and ride
on a roller coaster.

Downstairs I can hear Mum and Dad. I don't go down.

I go into my sister's room. I lie down under her bed.

The phone goes. Please don't answer it. Please don't answer it. Please don't answer it.

I go to bed at eight o'clock. I don't even watch much TV.

In the future people will look at me and they'll know I was right about all this. In the future people will do what I say. I'll be like a Führer. Do you think I'm joking? Do you think this is some kind of a joke?

I watch the TV with my sister all morning. She comes back from the tube station. She can't get to work. The images are from CCTV cameras close by to the scene. They change every thirty seconds. I watch them. I keep thinking something is going to happen. The people keep talking but the images only change every thirty seconds or so. I wonder what it's like down there. I wonder what it smells like. I think about the rats. It's such a hot day that I have to close the curtains to stop the sunlight glaring on the television.

I wish she was on the tube. Lisa. I wish Lisa had had a training day and happened to find herself sitting on a tube bound for the centre of town when a young man with a backpack climbed on.

The way the images move, I think the word is tantalising.

I look at my sister.

Are you laughing or are you crying?
What?
Are you laughing or are you crying?


*Images of hell.*
*They are silent.*

**Five**

Have you got any cigarettes?

I'm sorry?

Have you got a cigarette I could have?

Sure. Here.

Can I have the packet?

What?

Can I have your packet of cigarettes?

No, don't be –

Please.

How long are you staying?

Long enough. Don't worry.

I wasn't worried. Believe me.

You're looking well.

Thank you.

You've lost weight.

I have a bit.

You look rather dashing.

Dashing?

But you need to clean your house.

I know.

What room am I staying in?

In here. You can fold the sofa out.

Can't I sleep in your room?

Fuck off.

*You* could sleep on the sofa.

–

Put some music on.

What music do you want to hear?

You decide. Have you seen Mum and Dad?

Last month. I went up.

How are they?

They're fantastically well. Dad's taken up jogging. Mum keeps buying things. She's bought an array of electronic goods the like of which I've never even heard of.

Good Lord.

I know. Are you going to go and see them?

I might do. I might not. I might have other things to do. Have you got any booze?

No.

Get some.

Alcoholic.

Now.

*

You wanna know my favourite bit? This always happens. It's always hilarious. You'll see them talking about their loss. Maybe their child has been abducted. Or they lost a lover in a terrorist attack. Or a natural disaster. Or just, you know, in the general course of, of, of, of −

Life.

Of life, precisely. And they always do this! They'll be talking perfectly normally. They'll be talking with real grace and often they'll be, they'll be, it's like they'll be −

Happy?

Happy, yes. But then the thought of their lost one, of their child or their lover or their colleague, hits them like a train. And their voices catch in their throats and they can't carry on. Tears well up in their eyes. And what we do is, we stay with them. Every time. We hold them in our gaze for a good twenty seconds before the cut. It has become a formula. That, for me, is one of the highest achievements of our time.

Do you ever get tired?

And I love the way that certain phrases in our language
have become like a kind of intellectual Pepto-Bismol.
Language is used to constipate people's thinking. Yob
Culture. Binge Drinking. What do these things fucking
mean? What do they fucking mean exactly? We're losing all
sense of precision. Or accuracy. We're losing all sense of
language. And at the same time some of the fundamental
rights and fundamental privileges of our culture have been
removed from us.

Such as?

Simple joys.

Such as?

The simple joy of beating up your lover. The feeling you get
when you molest your own child. The desire to touch the
physically handicapped. Or a burn victim. Or the
blemished. That recoil you get, instinctively.

—

What?

—

What have I said?

\*

How did you sleep?

I slept incredibly well. I slept really deeply. I didn't have a
single dream. I closed my eyes. Opened them up again.
Eight hours had passed. It was fantastic.

Would you like some breakfast?

Yes I would, please.

What would you like?

I have absolutely no idea. Surprise me.

You look like you slept well.

You what?

You look rested.

Thank you.

You look great.

Thank you.

It's really good to see you.

Yeah. You too.

You were absolutely mad last night. But it is.

—

What do you want to do today?

Go out.

Where do you want to go?

*

She was a cleaner at St Pancras, at the train station. She found out she was pregnant. This was a hundred years ago. She came here. She spent all her money on getting a room. Threw herself over the side of the stairs. All the way down into the lobby. I've never seen her. People talk about her all the time. That's why they built the handrail.

How did you find out you could get in?

I was persistent.

It's amazing.

People reckon they've seen Roman soldiers marching through the basement. Or there's the man in Room 10.

Who's that?

There's a man who lurks around the back of one of the rooms here. Room 10. If you approach him he runs away. I've seen him. Loads of people have.

Did he run away from you?

Yeah.

He must be mad then.

–

–

They'll open this up. If the Olympics come here. They're gonna build the extension for the Channel Tunnel here. Join us all up to Europe. You'll be able to go anywhere. They'll re-open it. It's mine until then.

*

Keep your eyes open.

I am doing.

Any second.

–

–

–

There!

Wow!

It's for the British Museum. It's not been used for sixty years.

Fucking hell.

I know! They closed it because there was no need of it any more. With Holborn and Tottenham Court Road.

You can imagine the people.

I know.

Standing there.

–

–

The whole city's haunted. Every street there's something disused. There are forty tube stations, closed for fifty years. There are hundreds of pubs. There are hundreds of public toilets. The railway tracks. The canal system. The street map is a web of contradiction and complication and between each one there's a ghost.

—

People disappear here in ways they don't in other cities. People get buried in rooms. They get walled up in cellars. They're dug under the gardens. All of these things happen. What? What's funny? Don't you believe me?

Of course I believe you.

What then?

I'm just happy.

What are you happy about?

Seeing you. You idiot.

*

We didn't watch it.

No.

Any of it.

I know.

I bet it was fucking dreadful.

I would have liked to have seen Pink Floyd.

I would have rather cut my eyes out with a spoon.

I'm extremely drunk.

Me too.

—

—

Where were you?

What?

You never told me. All this time.

I was all over the place.

Tell me where.

No.

Why? Why won't you?

—

Were you all right?

—

Were you?

Not really.

Why not?

—

What happened?

You don't need to know.

I'm sorry.

What for?

I'm sorry you weren't all right. I would have done anything to have stopped you from getting hurt.

—

Come here.

—

You smell nice.

Thank you.

You smell like you. Nobody else smells like you. Why is that?

I have no idea.

*

In Moscow all the black marketeers and prostitutes were evacuated from the city centre to create an archetypal image of the dignity of Soviet communism. In Munich the Israeli wrestling team went to the theatre to watch *Fiddler on the Roof.* Moshe Weinberg, their coach, got so drunk with the actors afterwards that when the kidnap started he attacked one of Black September with a fruit knife. In Atlanta they flew the flag of the Confederacy from the roofs of most of the venues. In Barcelona trackside officers carried sub-machine guns. I fucking hope London doesn't get it. It'll rip the heart out of the East End. It'll be a catastrophe.

Shut up.

What?

Shut up. Stop fucking talking.

–

Here.

What?

Feel this.

–

Stop talking and feel this.

Where?

Here.

What about it?

It's soft, isn't it?

*

We shouldn't do this.

I know.

It's against every rule that has ever been written by anybody in the whole history of human culture.

I know.

You're my sister.

I know.

This is.

What?

I can't.

Come on.

I can't.

Please. For me. There. There. It feels good. Doesn't it? Well, doesn't it?

\*

Oranges.

Oranges?

Yeah. Or apples. Kiwi fruit, a bit.

I didn't know kiwi fruit *had* a smell.

It's a very subtle smell. You smell of it. Very subtly.

You smell of grass.

Grass like draw grass or grass like freshly cut grass?

Freshly cut grass.

Can I ask you something?

Of course.

Are you all right?

Yeah. I am. I'm fine.

—

You look about fifteen. In a good way. There's something about the light on your face.

Can I tell you something?

Go on.

I've wanted to do that for fucking ages.

Have you?

Years.

God.

I know.

What do we do now?

We could get something to eat. We could watch a video. Have you got any porn? We could watch some porn. I'd quite like to watch some porn, I think.

I don't.

We could download some.

Fuck off.

We could go for a walk. Go to Brick Lane and buy a bagel. Get a bottle of wine from the pub next door. I'll put your jeans on and go next door and get a bottle of wine and bring it back here and lie in bed and drink it with you. We could do that. What? Why are you smiling?

Cos I'm happy.

\*

Do they know you watch them, do you think?

I've no idea.

Do they ever watch you?

I don't know.

I wonder if they do.

They might do.

They might turn the lights off and lie in the dark and watch you work.

They might do.

Have you ever spoken to them?

No.

I wonder what they're like.

I bet they're cunts.

Don't say that. They might be lovely. What do you think they'd say?

If what?

If they saw us here.

They'd think you were my girlfriend.

What if they knew?

I don't know.

I am kind of your girlfriend, aren't I? A bit.

Kind of.

—

What did they say? At work?

They didn't say anything.

What did you tell them?

I told them you had food poisoning.

*

If I set you a task to do would you do it?

It depends what it is.

It shouldn't.

Well, it would. Don't push it.

If I set you one you could set me one.

Are you sure?

Absolutely.

I might set you a really terrible one.

I wouldn't care.

Or a really rude one.

That wouldn't matter. That would be good.

Go on then.

Take your top off.

Here?

Yeah.

There.

Drop to the floor.

To the floor?

To the ground. I want you to do some press-ups for me.

You what?

I want you drop to the ground and do ten press-ups for me.

—

Thank you. That was lovely.

My turn now.

*

I'm not telling you.

You have to.

I don't.

We made a deal.

It doesn't count.

Yes it does. Of course it does.

That wasn't what I was talking about.

I don't care. I did my press-ups for you. People watched me.
Strangers. You made me. You made those rules up. I make
the rules of what I want you to do.

I'll do anything else.

I don't want anything else. I want you to tell me what
happened.

No.

What happened to you?

No.

What happened to you?

I'm not –

What fucking happened?

Nothing happened. I went away. I thought things would be
better than they were. They weren't. I did some jobs. I got
my passport stolen. I came back home.

What kind of jobs?

Normal jobs. Jobs. Jobs for money. It was nothing. It wasn't
the jobs. It was the disappointment.

–

–

I don't think I understand you.

No.

—

Come to bed with me.

—

We can fuck all night if you want to. I'm not tired. Are you tired? I'm not tired at all. You could tell me all the things you ever wanted to do with me and we could do them and nobody would ever know. I love you so much it's like my body is bursting out of my skin and all I want is for you to love me in the same way and for it to be like this for ever. I know that it won't be.

No.

But that's what I want.

\*

I should go to work today.

Don't.

I don't want to. I have to go back. There are things I need to do.

What things?

There's a report we need to finish. By next week. Everybody else'll be working their arses off trying to finish it.

Are you not tired?

I'm all right.

Did you sleep?

I did a bit.

Did you see?

What?

London got the Olympics.

Fucking hell.

I know. The French are apoplectic.

We missed it.

I know.

How did we miss that?

I don't know.

It's awful.

I know.

—

Would you like some coffee?

I would please.

—

—

What would I have to do to stop you from going in?

Don't.

What would I have to promise you?

Nothing you promise me will make any difference.

Wouldn't it?

No.

I'll wait for you.

OK.

I'll stay in all day and watch TV and wait for you to come home.

OK.

I'll have your tea ready for you. I'll cook you something nice. I'll go to the shops and get something nice to cook. I'll get your Pink Floyd records out so you can listen to them to make up for the disappointment because everybody says they were brilliant according to this.

Right. That'd be nice.

Can I ask you something?

Go on.

Are you getting a bit frightened now?

*

I was worried about you. You're really late.

I know.

I was terrified. I tried ringing you but all the mobile phone lines were down.

I know. I'm sorry.

You're safe.

Yeah.

Where were you?

They cancelled all the tubes. I had to walk home.

Fucking hell.

What?

Just fucking hell. Fucking hell. Fucking hell.

—

I thought you were dead.

I wasn't.

No.

It's mad out there. Everybody's walking. All the pubs are packed.

—

You need to go.

—

I'm really sorry. You do.

What are you talking about?

You need to go. You need to leave. You can't stay here any more. This is awful. This is all awful. We have to stop doing this. There are some things which you just can't do and fucking hell did you not see the news at all?

Of course I did.

Did you not see what's going on?

What's that got to do with anything?

I can't do this any more. This is all wrong. It's terrible. What are you even doing here? I look at you and all I can see is your stupid fucking horrible fucking face.

Stop it.

I walked home and the place has been destroyed. And I come home to this. And I can't bear it any more and I want it to stop.

I'll kill myself.

I don't believe you.

*

This isn't the last time I'll see you. I will see you again. We will see each other again.

—

I'll tell Mum and Dad you had to go. That it was good to see you. You asked after them. You wanted to see them and then you had to go.

I don't know what I'm going to do without you.

You'll be – People survive. You'll be all right.

You've completely broken my heart.

There are some things that people don't recover from but sadness is never one of them.

It's not about being sad. It's not that I'm sad. For Christ's sake!

No. Sorry.

How long do you think we should wait?

You what?

Until we see each other again. How long do you think we should leave it?

I have no idea.

How long do you think it'll take?

Hundreds and hundreds and hundreds and hundreds of years.

Yeah.

I think about you all the time.

–

I close my eyes and all I ever see is you and your hair and your face and that's not a healthy thing for anybody.

–

You're my sister.

Yeah.

–

–

Have you got everything?

Yes. I think so.

–

–

If you've left anything where should I send it? Is there an address I could send it to?

Throw it away. Put it on eBay. Keep it.

*Images of hell.*
*They are silent.*

**Four**

It's dark. It's still dark when I leave my house.

I kiss my children goodbye. I kiss my wife. I promise that I'll call her.

There's nobody around.

There's the sound of my feet on the gravel of my driveway. The metal on my front gate is cold to touch. My bag slices into my shoulders.

The bus driver turns his face to the road. He's the only vehicle on the road at this time of the morning. He's the only person here.

A young Bangladeshi boy with a Walkman slumps in the middle of the bus towards the right-hand side. Stares out of the window. His feet are rested on the seat in front of him. I sit on the other side. Behind him. I watch the back of his head. I watch his gentle movements to the sound of his Walkman. I take aim. I release the safety catch. I stare down the barrel, down my arm, rigid, straight. I squeeze. I pick up a copy of the morning *Metro*. I look for my horoscopes. I've always looked for my horoscopes.

As we bore into its heart, though, the traffic thickens. There are more buses. Heavy goods vehicles pack up after midnight deliveries. Rumble away again. Lone drivers with no passengers understand the idea of the car pool. They admire the idea of the car pool. They are determined to get involved in a car pool.

They rub eyes with hands balancing coffee in paper cups. Warning. Contents are extremely hot.

We swing round the turnings of the one-way system. I send psychic signals to the bus driver. Drive through the red lights. Turn right on the left turn only. Drive up and over the pavements. From today, from now on you can do, you have it in you to do whatever it is that you want to do. Here is where the rules end. Today is the day when the law stops working.

I thank the bus driver when I get off the bus. I always thank the bus driver when I get off the bus. He doesn't say anything. He stares out of his windscreen. His eyes don't move at all.

I turn out of and away from Piccadilly Gardens.

I climb up the hill towards the railway station.

I could do with a coffee.

I really need a cup of coffee.

Can I have a cup of coffee please? Thank you. Great. Thanks. Thank you.

All of a sudden, as if by magic, there are people everywhere. Turning away from train platforms. Suited and smart and elegant and crisp. Weary-eyed and bloated. Breakfasting on McDonald's or Breakfast Bars or Honey and Granola. Lugging their laptops. Clicking their heels. Pulling their shirt cuffs. Pressing their phones. They've been working all night on a polish. They've been driven by the R&D. Their attention to detail and their R&D is breathtaking.

We have reserved seats in different carriages.

We don't check that each other is here. We don't need to check that each other is here. We trust one another. We're here.

The train arriving on Platform 5 is the 5.43 for London Euston. Calling at Stockport, Macclesfield, Stoke-on-Trent, Milton Keynes Central and London Euston only.

We will take the train to Stoke and get off at Stoke.

From Stoke we will take a train to Derby and change at Derby.

From Derby we will take a train to King's Cross St Pancras.

At King's Cross St Pancras we will each travel on a different tube line. At King's Cross St Pancras one of us will take a Piccadilly Line to Heathrow. One of us will take a Victoria Line to Brixton. One of us will take a Hammersmith and City Line train to Hammersmith. At King's Cross St Pancras I am going to take a Circle Line train via Liverpool Street. We won't speak. We won't signal with one another. We will not communicate with one another in any way. We will, however, each send one text.

I think the weather is warming up. I think we're going to have a beautiful day today. Today the sun will shine all throughout England.

The luggage racks are spacious. They have space for my backpack. There's plenty of room.

This is the first train. There are only a handful of people on my carriage.

And when the second of our number comes into my carriage and sees me he walks right through the carriage and away from me into a carriage further down the train. And we don't speak. And we don't look at one another. We don't say anything at all.

A man sat across the table from me has removed his tie. He furrows his brow at an early-morning anagram, seven across, eight letters, second letter E. He looks like –

I drink bad black coffee from Upper Crust. I am very much in need of mineral water. There are no almond croissants.

I want an almond croissant. Where the fuck are your almond croissants, you fucking bewigged, myopic, prurient, sexless dead?

A man down the carriage from me. A young man. He is dressed smartly. He is handsome. He won't stop picking his nose. He burrows around in his nose, removes something from it and surreptitiously, imagining that nobody can see him, slips it into his mouth. Toys with it between his teeth.

By the sides of the tracks as we pull out of Manchester and Stockport there is a mass of containers. There are corrugated-steel industrial units.

I look into the eyes of the woman sat across the seat from me. I think for a second that she's been crying. She hasn't. It's my imagination.

The sunshine through the window of the train is burning up my arms. I want to take my jacket off. Can I take my jacket off please?

I close my eyes for a time. I can sleep now. I try to sleep.

I wake up and panic about how far we've come. I look out of my window as we pull out of Macclesfield.

I've forgotten to do something. There is definitely something that I've forgotten, I've forgotten, can you help me, is there something that I've forgotten? I think it's a word. Is it a word?

I honestly have no memory of changing trains at Stoke. I must have changed trains at Stoke.

East. Out towards Derby.

Disused Jet garage forecourts sit side by side with double driveways. Here there are food-makers and the food they make is chemical. It fattens the teenage and soaks up the pre-teen. Nine-year-old children all dazzled up in boob tubes and mini-skirts and spangly eyeliner as fat as little pigs stare out of the windows of family estate cars. In the sunshine of mid-morning in the suburbs of the South Midlands heroin has never tasted so good. Internet sex contact pages have never seemed more alluring. Nine hundred television channels have never seemed more urgent. And everybody needs an iPod. And nobody can ever get a *Metro* any more.

If I had the power I would take a bomb to all of this. To every grazing horse and every corrugated-metal shed and every wind-blasted tree and every telephone mast and every graveyard. Wipe it all off the skin of the world. Scratch it away.

The only thing I remember about the station at Derby, as we wait at four different points, staring in four different directions, is the oddness of a unisex hairdresser's being there, at the station. Nobody today is having a haircut.

I climb on the third train. Try to close my eyes again. I daren't.

The land rolls on.

I'd like to listen to some music. I'd very much like to listen to the music of Pink Floyd. There's a woman across the aisle from me. She is dressed in a black business suit. She is wearing black tights. I'd very much like to lie in her bed on a Sunday morning eating oven-heated croissants and listening to the music of Pink Floyd.

The teenage girls on the counter of Boots didn't even check the signature on my card. Five hundred bottles of peroxide for hair dye. Fifty bottles of nail varnish remover. I'm making a movie. I'm the runner on a movie.

I want some chewing gum. I want to read the sports pages of a national newspaper.

We're getting closer now. You can tell it. In the shape of the land here.

Glass and concrete and grey metal tubes pepper platforms, punctured by yellow paint at Luton Airport Parkway.

Aeroplanes fly throughout the whole of Europe. Don't forget the tax. Don't forget the air tax. Don't forget the consequence. An array of suburbs all throughout Europe have been re-energised by the possibility of cheap flights. There is a legacy of incremental deep-vein thrombosis and an explosion of ramp attendants. Asian boys from suburbs the whole of Europe over have become ramp attendants. Juggling the matrix snake of the luggage hold. Perfecting the ergonomics of bags on wheels. Their mothers package sandwiches in airtight silver foil. Their sisters spray perfume. Their fathers drive buses that move you from one car park to another. Welcome to England.

London rises. It takes you by surprise. Cut out of the edges of bomb blasts. And a thousand years of fire. This is a city that is always on fire. This is a city that is forever under attack.

Nobody checks my ticket. The ticket guards stare at one another's shoes, giggling.

St Pancras Hotel is a spectre from another time. The whole of the city looms up and over us through the St Pancras Hotel. A metal stairway and the sweep of elegance. Haunted by women who have walked down the stairwell.

There are things I need to say. There is a sequence of words that I've been told I must say. But I can't remember what order it goes in. I want to phone home. I want to tell my wife to wake up and take our children to school. I want to ask her what order the sequence of words is meant to go in.

There is a panelled walkway from St Pancras to the Underground. There are blue arrows telling me to go this way only. I can't seem to feel the weight of my bag any more and I'm terrified that something has gone wrong. Something has gone wrong here. Something terrible has gone wrong.

I follow the blue lines in that way only.

They apologise for any inconvenience that anything may have caused. There is a constant state of apology for any inconvenience that may have been caused.

They have dug up the floor tiles. They are rebuilding everything. They have no choice but to rebuild everything. When the Olympics get here this place will have the newest floor tiles you'll be able to imagine. All of the newspaper headlines, each after the other after the other, are roaring with delight. They cannot believe what happened yesterday. Nobody can believe what happened yesterday and what that will mean.

I pay £2.20 for a single ticket to Zone 2 via Zone 1 stations.

I smile at the man who holds the gate to the platform open for me so that I can get through with my bag. But he doesn't smile back. He doesn't check my ticket. He doesn't even look at me. He looks away from me.

The second of our number sends me a text message. The third of our number sends me a text message. The first of our number sends me a text message. I reply to them all.

I follow the signs for the Circle Line. The platform is busy. The platform is busier than I expected it to be. I find the space for the busiest carriage. At the heart of the train. I have to push my way on with my bag. People are complaining about the size of my bag.

Suddenly I feel lighter than I have ever felt in my whole life.

We move past Farringdon. Where the platform is open and sunk in the grey blue light of morning. And red-brick Moorgate. Liverpool Street is white with sugar and pace and desire. Smoke blue, blood red, ghost white.

The train pulls out of Liverpool Street and moves towards Aldgate.

## Three

You look just like him.

That's not true.

You've got the same eyes. You've got exactly the same hair. How old is he?

He's twenty-five.

He's very handsome.

I worry about him constantly.

What do you worry about?

I worry that he won't achieve the things he has the potential to achieve. I worry that nobody will ever fall in love with him. That he won't get out of bed. Ever. That he'll die before me. Things like that.

Solipsist.

He is incredibly vulnerable. He has absurdly soft skin, for a man of his age. Did you call me a solipsist?

You are.

I'm not in the least bit solipsistic. I'm not a solipsist at all.

You're projecting onto him. Mercilessly.

That's not true. It's the opposite of that.

Would you like another drink?

I'm not sure now.

Are you all grumpy and cross now?

I'm just not sure if I want to be insulted by you.

It's incredibly good to see you.

I was going to say that it's good to see you too. Until you started insulting me.

You're looking fantastic. You funny little man. You've lost weight. Your skin's cleared up.

My skin?

I remember your skin being kind of blotchy. We used to stare at it during your seminars.

Did you?

It isn't now.

Who stared at me?

All of us. It looks fresh now. You look good.

Thank you.

That's my pleasure.

I think I would like another drink. I think I'd like another Merlot.

I bet you would.

Will you buy me another Merlot please?

It's funny, isn't it?

What is?

People's faces. When people get older their faces don't change. They just decay a little bit. The shape is the same, though. The shape of their eyes. You recognise them completely. They send off little messages through your synapses.

Your face has changed. Your eyes have got smaller. How did that happen?

I have no idea. It's the same with voices, by the way. The speed with which we recognise one another's voices when we pick up our telephones is staggering to me. Human beings are so fucking clever that sometimes it makes me want to fall over.

Should I go myself, to get my drink?

Don't you think I'm funny?

No.

I am. I think I am. I make myself laugh my head off. Wait here.

*

I went to America.

Good thinking.

I got myself a job in a faculty in Minneapolis.

What was Minneapolis like?

It was fantastically cold. You go outside in winter and after seconds, literally seconds, your nasal hairs freeze over. That was unusual.

It sounds it.

The students were banal. They all had the same haircut, which disconcerted me. And everybody was fat. You had to walk for twenty minutes to get any fresh fruit. Even then it was coated in genetically modified chemical additive.

How long were you there for?

Two years. I found it difficult to get the energy to leave. I blame the diet.

And how long have you been back?

Four years.

Four years?

Yeah.

Jesus.

What?

When did you graduate?

Eight years ago.

I'm nearly literally twice your age.

Yeah.

That makes me feel terrible. That makes me feel like I'll probably die soon.

You might.

Well, yes. I might. We all might. Anybody might. But I probably will. Is my point.

I enjoyed the teaching.

Did you?

I want to teach again.

–

–

That's where I come in.

No.

No?

I mean maybe. I mean yes. Really I mean yes.

You don't sound like you enjoyed the teaching.

I did. I just didn't enjoy the students. I hankered after British students. I kept imagining how great British students would be.

They're not.

I bet they fucking are. I need a job.

Yeah. We all need a job.

I can't work in bars again. I'm far too old to get a bar job. It would be so humiliating.

You can't even remember to get people drinks.

No.

I'll see what I can do.

—

I'll talk to the Dean. I have no idea if there's anything available.

Thank you.

That's OK.

This is my grateful face. This is my excited face. This is my excited and grateful face.

They're remarkable.

I know. Have you eaten?

What?

Supper. Have you had any supper?

No.

No. Neither have I.

*

It gets to a point in a marriage where the house is full of these horrible psychic forces. You can feel the anger. I'd come into the house and look at her standing in the living room or in our bedroom and there would be part of me that would want to cave her head in with a brick. That's quite an unnerving feeling.

You should have left each other earlier than you did by the sound of things.

There was Mark. I didn't want to leave while he was still living there.

No.

—

Do you like living on your own?

I do. You know? I do. I do. I do. I really do. I like shopping for food. I like discovering food shops in odd places and going there. I like eating out occasionally on my own. Going to the cinema and not worrying about being back in time. Going to the pub and staying there. Working all night if I want to. Naked. At my desk. Scratching my balls.

Lovely.

I know. And I've started running.

Have you?

I've taken up jogging.

I thought you'd lost weight.

I love it. Round the park. I did four laps on Saturday. I'm going to enter the Olympics, I think.

You should.

I will.

—

What do you think that'll be like?

What?

The Olympics.

I have no idea.

Don't you think it'll be rather brilliant?

I'm not sure.

I was in my car this afternoon, when they announced it. I had the radio on. And the hosts of the Olympic Games in 2012 will be . . . London! I punched my fists in the air. I nearly punched the roof off the car. I honked my horn in celebration. Other people did too. It was like we were having a big party on the road, in our cars. Everybody was grinning at each other.

I didn't really know what to think.

Oh come on! You know? Life is so short.

*

Are you not cold?

No.

Would you like to borrow my scarf?

—

What?

Nothing.

—

I used to come here when I was a child. To the museum. Have you ever been in there?

No.

You should go in. There are dolls in there from four hundred years ago. Other dolls, porcelain dolls from the nineteenth century with three faces. They're terrifying. I'll take you.

Will you?

You get me a job and I'll bring you to the museum and show you the dolls with the three faces.

Would you like some coffee?

I'm sorry?

Would you like to come in and have a cup of coffee with me?

*

It's from Jamaica.

Right.

From Blue Mountain. It's the most exclusive coffee in the world. How do you like that?

Very flash.

What do you think?

It's lovely. Thank you.

Good. Good. I'm glad.

I like your flat.

Do you?

I do. It's simple. It's spare. It's minimalist.

There's nothing here, you mean.

It feels deliberate.

It isn't.

That's not the point. I like the view. You can see the Gherkin.

Yes. I rather like that. Would you like to stay?

I'm sorry?

Here. Tonight.

–

I don't mean to 'stay' stay. I mean. I've got the room. And it's late. It'd be difficult for you to get back now. You'd have to get the night bus. And the night bus from here is like one of the lower circles of hell. You'd never survive it.

–

I'd make you breakfast.

–

It's been very good to see you. I'm sorry. I shouldn't have asked.

–

–

You had no idea, of course, at the time. But you were
everything to me. You were my teacher. I was completely
besotted with you. I wanted you, what I wanted you to do
was, I wanted you to notice me. Of course you never did.
You shouldn't have asked me. No. You probably really
shouldn't.

*

The sheets are completely untouched. They're practically
brand new.

Thank you.

Have you got some pyjamas?

Pyjamas?

You can borrow some. If you need to. I've got piles and
piles of the things.

Thank you.

What time do you need to get up in the morning?

I don't really need . . . I'm not working at the moment.

I get up absurdly early. I have completely lost the ability to
sleep any more. So I'll wake you up at any time you want.

Nine o'clock. How's nine o'clock. Is that all right?

A lie-in!

Kind of.

–

–

It'll be quite funny wearing your pyjamas.

Funny?

I've not worn pyjamas for years. Not since I was a little girl.

–

What?

Can I ask you something?

Of course.

Will you dance with me?

—

If I put some music on. Would you dance with me?

*

Are you crying?

What?

I couldn't tell if you were laughing or if you were crying.

Shhhh.

Hey. Hey. Don't cry.

I'm not.

Hey.

—

—

—

Don't.

Shhhh.

Don't, please.

Shhhhh.

Please don't.

Come on.

—

I can feel you breathing.

Please don't.

You know exactly what you're doing to me. You've known all night what you've been doing to me.

–

What knickers are you wearing? Tell me.

Be quiet.

Are you even wearing any?

Christ.

Come on. I'm noticing you. This is me noticing you.

–

Ow.

–

Ow. You fucking. You. That fucking hurt.

–

I should beat the crap out of you for doing that.

–

Don't tell me that you didn't want exactly what –

Is there a lock on that door?

What?

Is there a lock on the bedroom door?

–

Can it be locked from the inside?

Yes. Of course it can.

I need to sleep somewhere.

–

–

–

You're quite little, aren't you?

Little?

I've never noticed before.

                    *

I'm very sorry. For what I did last night. I was awful.

It's not enough.

No. Of course not.

–

I made you some breakfast. I cooked bacon and everything.
Will you stay for breakfast? Will you stay for breakfast,
please?

–

–

I need to get to Edgware Road. Can I get the train to
Edgware Road from near here?

I dreamt about you last night. It was horrible. The dream
was horrible.

–

I woke up. I thought my wife was there. I thought she was
sleeping next to me. She looks like Mark when she's asleep.
She wasn't. I was on my own. I'm fucking cracking up is the
thing. I'm completely losing my fucking mind.


**Two**

You never get bus conductors any more. On some tube lines
now you don't even get drivers. The machines have started
to run themselves.

I like this.

I have absolutely no interest in speaking to anybody.

In the free newspaper there is talk of the events of the weekend. They write, in this paper, without any editorial bias. I hate the fucking thing. They've removed any semblance of perspective or personality.

This was not music. What they did on Saturday was the opposite of music. It was everything I wish I had the strength to rip down and destroy. I'd take a pickaxe to the lot of them. They manifest charity masquerading as action. They are driven by a singular spirit of self-congratulation. It makes me want to bite the throats out of their domestic pets.

I have an article to deliver.

I take the bus to the entrance of the faculty. Walk up Gower Street. The university brackets the road with the hospital. Right through the northern heart of central London. One starts in one bracket. Crosses. Returns.

I haven't worked there, properly, for fifteen years now. They look at me with a mix of bewilderment, pity and an odd kind of rage. I leave my article for Dr Schults. He'll call me.

I go back home.

There was a time when I'd walk. Gower Street to Hammersmith.

I couldn't do it any more. I can barely fucking breathe half the time.

Wait for the bus. Get the bus. Get home. Drink tea. Try not to spend too many hours staring out of the window. If you stare long enough into a mirror, of course, you begin to hallucinate. My entire life has the feeling of that nowadays.

I watch television with a mixture of awe and horror.

Sometimes I forget if I've eaten or not. It is as likely that this will lead to me eating two meals of an evening as it is that

I'll end up eating none. I wouldn't be at all surprised if I
became enormously fat.

I don't see anybody. I don't speak to anybody. And God,
the fucking horror if I were forced to. I wouldn't know what
to do with my hands. Occasionally letters are delivered.
Letters from abroad that may require a signature. I go to
the door. I swear that they can see it in my eyes. The blank
shivering terror.

Where do I sign?

Do you need a date with that?

Do you need the time of delivery to be recorded?

Would you like to come in for a cup of tea?

There are few things that have caused me more pleasure in
recent years than the coverage of the war in Iraq. This offers
me the same kind of thrills as do exciting video games.
There was a time when I played video games quite often.
The feeling I get watching war coverage is the same.

In the evenings I wear my husband's robe. Most of his
clothes were wrapped by his sister into black bin liners and
taken away to a variety of shops. His robe was saved. I pull
the blinds down. And I turn the computer on. Sometimes I
don't pull the blinds down. Sometimes I like the idea that in
the middle of the night, in the heart of west London, all of
the neighbours can see me. His gown is, it's this red, silk
gown. I let my hand fall beneath it.

I watch the trailers. Every trailer follows a genre convention.
There's a moment, at the end of every film, where the girl is
waiting for the boy to come. Kneeling below him. Looking
up. She asks him to come on her face. And at that moment
she looks tired and worn out and the good years, when the
work was flying in, have taken their toll. And you do kind of
think.

Dr Schults doesn't ring me. He doesn't ring me to tell me he got the article. He doesn't email. He doesn't acknowledge it in any way.

I lose complete track of when I go to bed.

I have the same thing for breakfast every day. I have a hundred grams of muesli mixed with fifty grams of fresh berries and milk and honey and yogurt. I have some fresh orange juice and some coffee. And then I go up to my desk and I start to work.

And in between jobs. When an article is finished and there are no new commissions waiting to begin I can sit at my screen and I simply have no idea what to do. And the pull, my God, the pull towards the world that is there, on the other side of my screen!

I have to leave in the end. To go shopping. To buy ingredients to make some food. To go into town. To go to a museum. To do anything I possibly can to get away from my computer.

I hate shopping for my own food. I see other people in food shops and they fill me with the deadness of real despair. What is the point of buying aubergines when there are people in the world who dress like that? And who have faces like that? And talk with accents like that? And treat their children like that?

In town everybody's talking about the possibility that the Olympic Games might be coming to London. I'm struck by the irony of this. Because the people of London, palpably to me, are universally obese and under-exercised. Fat fuckers. Gibbering about athletes. The lot of them.

She's dressed in a baby-doll nightie. With a red eye mask over the top of her face. And she asks him if he's her daddy. Call me Daddy. Will you call me Daddy? And it doesn't bother me. It doesn't matter to me how old she is.

Two days pass like this.

There are images of things that I have seen seared onto the inside of my skull.

And then on Wednesday lunchtime the news comes in that London's bid to host the Olympics in 2012 has been successful. And now people smile. Transistor radios broadcast the events over and over. We go live to Trafalgar Square. We go live to Singapore where Lord Coe is speaking. We go live to the derelict battered crack dens of Stratford where residents there can barely contain their glee at the prospect of Kelly Holmes racing madly around the peripheries of their houses.

Cars do little dances. Drivers toot their horns at one another with idiot inane grins on their faces. Shocked by their own daring. Epileptic with thoughts of how old they'll be in 2012.

And when I get back Dr Schults has called. He's left a message for me on my phone. This is BT Call Minder 1571. The person you are calling is not available. Please leave a message after the tone.

I listen to the message three times. Put some music on. Pour myself a whisky. Pour myself another. I smoke an entire packet of cigarettes in one sitting.

What I realise now is that I won't die. I'm going to live on and on.

He wants me to see him the next day. He wants me to go in and see him the next morning to talk about things.

I don't sleep.

At three o'clock in the morning I go outside into the garden. This city is never silent. At this time of morning it hums and roars in the distance. It has a throb and a pulse of its own. It feels latent. It feels charged. It feels sprung. As though something remarkable is going to happen.

I go back to bed eventually. I have no idea what time it is.

I am eighty-three years old next month.

I get up. Measure out my breakfast. Get dressed. Get on the tube. Go and see Daniel.

But it's clear by the time I get to the tube station that something is going wrong. Nobody says anything. But Hammersmith tube station is closed. Both stations actually. For all three lines. On each side of the roundabout.

The traffic into town has stopped completely still.

Posters warn me not to make any journeys unless they're completely necessary.

I walk.

I walk through Hammersmith up towards Shepherd's Bush. Up Holland Park Road on to Notting Hill Gate. Down Notting Hill Gate up to the corner of the park. Down Oxford Street to Tottenham Court Road. Up Tottenham Court Road towards Gower Street. I'm very late. There's nobody there. Nobody came in today. Nobody at all came into the centre of London today. Nobody rang to let me know.

On my way back my feet, I think, start to blister and it feels like they might start bleeding.

There are masses of people waiting at bus stops. I see one man. He does look like my husband. Just for a second I was thrown. But he's far too young. He can't be more than forty. Did he see me looking at him? Did I frighten him? Did I frighten you? Were you frightened? I didn't mean to frighten you.

It's on days like this that I realise how intelligent my decision to talk you out of having children was. I mean, can you imagine? Really. Can you imagine what would have happened?

And tonight, I think, everybody in London walked home.

It's getting dark by the time I get back. As I approach my house the streets get smaller and they are quieter. I can't feel my feet any more. I think my socks have stuck to the soles of my feet.

It's a warm evening. There is the noise of music coming from one of the houses. People are listening to music of some description. And somebody close by is having a barbecue.

I can smell chicken. I can smell barbecued chicken cooking. It smells good.

It's nine o'clock.

I find the house where the chicken is being cooked and I knock on the door.

Hello.

– Can I help you?

I, I, I, I'm sorry.

– Can I, is there anything – ?

I walked past your house. I could smell chicken.

– What?

It smells delicious.

– We're having a barbecue. I'm sorry. Can I help you?

Can I have some?

– Can you – ?

I just wanted you to know that I think your chicken smells delicious.

– Thank you. You said.

And I wondered what would happen if I just knocked on your door and said, your chicken smells delicious, please can I have some of it?

– Ha.

Don't laugh.

– That's quite funny to me.

Don't laugh at me.

– How old are you?

What?

– You're completely fucking retarded, sweetheart, aren't you?

Don't laugh at me.

– Here.

What?

– Wait here. Don't come in.

–

–

–

–

–

–

–

– Here.

Thank you.

– I don't have any napkins. I'm sorry.

No. No. No. No. This is fine. This is kind of you. This is lovely. Thank you.

– I'd have brought you a beer but I decided not to.

No. I don't want a beer. I just wanted some chicken. I just wanted – This is lovely. Thank you.

I walk home. The chicken tastes good. I let myself in. I can't feel my feet any more. I can't understand why there are

tears pouring down the sides of my face. This makes
absolutely no sense to me at all.

*On the evening of 7 July 2005 many of the working people of London
walk home from their workplaces in the centre of the city.*

*Images of hell.*
*They are silent.*

## One

1  A church deacon, he was a man known for his deeply
held Christian faith and tolerance of other religions.

2  She usually drove to her PA job while her boyfriend
preferred to cycle from their home in Tottenham, north
London.

3  He had just moved in with his boyfriend of three years
but also spent much of his time looking after his
widowed mother, who suffers from multiple sclerosis.

4  Her daughter had just arrived in London from Poland
on the day her mother was killed.

5  He was passionate about two things: his family and
sport.

6  If he was known for anything, it was for his sense of fun.
If there was a party to go to or an occasion to celebrate,
he would always be the first and the loudest there.

7  Even in this time of sadness, friends tend to laugh when
discussing his life. It happens when they talk of his
passionate defence of all things Arsenal, should anyone
have dared mock his much-loved football club.

8   She came to Britain five years ago from Mauritius.

9   One of three sisters from a distinguished Italian family, she was preparing for a great celebration in Rome which would have united Catholic and Muslim rites.

10   She was making her daily journey to University College Hospital where she worked as an administrator in the neuroradiology department when she boarded the Piccadilly Line train on 7 July.

11   He was on his way to the Royal Borough of Kensington and Chelsea, where he worked as a human resources systems development officer.

12   He was on his way to a one-day course at the Kensington branch of Jessops, the camera chain. He sent a text message to his mother twenty-one minutes before the first blast, and that was the last his parents heard from him.

13   The twenty-six-year-old, an engineering executive from Hendon, was killed on the number 30 bus after he was evacuated from King's Cross.

14   His hit calypso is still played on local radio station ZJB, many years after it was recorded. But calypso was merely his hobby, albeit a highly acclaimed one.

15   When he was a teenager, his father caught him putting on his sister's heavy black mascara. He was going through a goth phase and had dyed his hair to match.

16   She was due to leave London on the evening of 7 July for a romantic long weekend in Paris with her boyfriend. The day before she died, her dad was wallpapering the kitchen, and she scrawled the words '06/07/05 we got the Olympic bid 2012 on this day' on the bare wall.

17   His hobbies included waterskiing, quad-bike riding and skiing. He had a lifelong love of music and met his fiancée, seven years ago, in a rock club.

18  He helped to set up the Ipswich and East Suffolk hockey club nine years ago.

19  She had taken leave from her job with a Turkish textile company to improve her English.

20  He was former chairman of the Polish Solidarity Campaign of Great Britain, vice chairman of the Havering branch of the Humanist Society, chairman of the H.G. Wells Society and a long-standing supporter of the Anti-Slavery Society, among other charities.

21  She had just sent text messages to friends telling them she had been safely evacuated from the tube. As well as travelling and socialising she loved music, and recently went to see Coldplay in Thailand.

22  She worked for BBC Books and the *Sun* for a short time.

23  She had lived in Luton for twenty-five years.

24  She attended the mosque every Friday, but loved Western culture and fashions and regularly shopped for designer clothes, shoes and handbags. She worked as a cashier at the Co-operative Bank in Islington.

25  She was evacuated from the Underground at Euston and decided to catch a bus to work.

26  Deciding that university was not for her, she moved to Salamanca for a year to learn Spanish. Her first job was in the wine trade, which took her abroad again, to Australia, where she lived in Melbourne for a year.

27  He travelled all over Europe as a product technical manager for the clothes manufacturers Burberry.

28  She had a successful career as an accountant in Glasgow and later the City, but she was as happy helping out at homeless hostels as she was discussing the financing of management buyouts.

29  Her taxi-driver husband described her as a 'devoted and much-loved wife and mother of two sons'.

30   He survived fleeing Vietnam as one of the boat people when he was less than a year old.

31   She was born in Auckland, New Zealand.

32   He was born in Vietnam, the son of a South Vietnamese soldier killed in the conflict when he was just five months old.

33   On a normal day, a politics graduate from Warwick University, he would have used a completely different route to his place of work.

34   There, on a website he helped create, hundreds of people have posted almost 18,000 words of tribute.

35   She was born in Tehran but made her home in London twenty years ago.

36   One of the last tasks she completed, with her usual cheerful verve, was promoting a new rose at Hampton Court flower show, named in honour of the Brownies on their ninetieth anniversary.

37   She was an optimist. Her mother is certain she would have taken comfort in the compassion and care shown to her family over the past fortnight.

38   She had lived in London for eighteen years and was nervous about visiting her native Israel because of the risk of suicide bus bombings.

39   She missed London; the people, the lifestyle, the pubs. So, after completing a two-year dental technology degree at the Los Angeles City College, she turned down an offer to continue her studies at the prestigious UCLA and returned to her adopted home town.

40   On any given Thursday night, she could be found at Chiquito in Staples Corner, the Mexican restaurant of choice for nights out with her friends Nell Raut and Andrea Cummings.

41  He was the kind of man people went to with their problems. 'He always had time to listen,' said his father.

42  His parents were killed by the Taliban when he was a teenager. He left his family in Afghanistan and arrived in Britain in January 2002 and was granted exceptional leave to stay. He was the only Afghan national to be killed in the bombings, and the last of the victims to be formally identified.

43  –

44  When he went on a three-month trip around Ghana, Senegal and Mali last year, he was satisfying a long-held ambition.

45  In 2003, she joined the specialist criminal law firm Reynolds Dawson as an assistant solicitor and worked as a duty solicitor in court and police stations, specialising in fraud and extradition.

46  She came to London earlier this summer to get a taste of big city life.

47  She was full of high hopes when she gave her mother her usual goodbye kiss at Liverpool Street. Mother and daughter always caught the same train from Billericay and had developed the fond little ritual as they went their separate ways. Ms Taylor had just heard that her temporary contract as a finance officer at the Royal Society of Arts in the Strand had been made permanent.

48  She dedicated her life to helping children as a radiographer.

49  She was a personal assistant who lived with her partner in Islington, north London.

50  Coming to Britain from Ghana in the mid-1980s was almost an accident for her. The Lebanese bank manager she worked for in her home town was forced to move to London for his son's medical treatment and

Mrs Wyndowa travelled with him to care for the family. When they returned to Lebanon, she remained in the UK, where she had made a new life.

51   He followed the same routine on the way to work every day for ten years. After leaving home shortly before 8 a.m., the IT specialist would take the tube to Liverpool Street, where he would join the early-morning regulars at Leonidas Belgian chocolate shop for a double espresso at 8.30 a.m. After half an hour quietly listening to others holding forth he would make the short walk to the offices of Equitas Holdings in St Mary Axe, where he worked.

52   Determined to improve his English, he headed for London shortly after gaining an IT engineering degree from the University Institute of Technology (IUT) in Saint-Martin-d'Hères, near Grenoble. He shared a flat in Kensal Green with three friends and worked in a pizza takeaway. He sent any spare money home to his younger sister but managed to save enough from his modest wages to buy a computer.

# Sea Wall

*Sea Wall* was first performed at the Bush Theatre, London, on 6 October 2008 with the following cast:

**Alex**                                    Andrew Scott

*Director*   George Perrin
*Designer*   Lucy Osborne
*Lighting*   Natasha Chivers
*Sound*   Emma Laxton
*Composer*   Arthur Darvill

## Characters

**Alex**, *thirty-one*

This monologue should be performed as far as possible on
a bare stage, as far as possible in natural light and as far as
possible without sound effects. Alex addresses the audience
directly.

Arthur
| (grandad)

Alex ⊤ Helen
(me)   |   (wife)

Lucy
(daughter)

**Alex**   She had us, both of us, absolutely round her finger. Fundamentally she achieved this through the way she looked at us. It shouldn't have been a surprise that the way she moved her head to one side should leave me basically on my knees or more akin, I should say, to a slightly tepid pool of just water, but what was more surprising was the effect it had on him.

Anything she wanted he gave to her. Anything she demanded he agreed to. And he agreed to everything with this same little smile on his face. The smile of a man who in actual fact was little more than four years old. I'm not saying I wouldn't have agreed to the same and more in his position, but it just seemed in some way more, what? Downright surprising? Coming from him.

He wasn't that kind of man. He was a soldier. When I say 'was', I mean was. I mean he used to be. Between 1968 and 1984 he was a soldier in the British infantry. He reached the rank of Lieutenant Colonel. He did five tours of Northern Ireland. And this was when, you know, doing a tour of Northern Ireland was more than just a few games of pool and a chat with some kids outside a fish and chip shop. Some of the photographs he took.

He used to have a Polaroid camera and some of the things that, after ʼ ʼd had a few drinks, he'd get out of his box to show me. You wouldn't have thought they were of Northern Ireland. There was something about them that I found in some way, you know, surprising.

He always refused to talk about South Georgia. Never mentioned it. I asked him about it one time and his face turned, within the matter of a few seconds, literally grey. Slate grey.

And even when he eventually retired from the army he retrained as a maths teacher for Christ's sake! I would have liked to have seen him teach. I can imagine the kind of teacher he was. I don't think he would have worn many

(1) Grandad.

cords. I don't think he would have shared too many coffees with the sixth-formers.

Come and play with me. Read me a story. Can I sit on your lap? Where's Grandpops? Oh! There he is. Not his kind of, scene, you know? But he did it with her.

(2) How to photograph

The first thing I learned about photography I learned when I was a kid. If you're taking a portrait photograph, if you possibly can, then take it from below the subject. It renders the subject actually oddly, what it does is it renders them not more heroic, not more godlike, oddly it renders them more human. And if you can take it in natural light, if you can capture the way the light falls, at the start of or at the end of a day especially, then it can be –

(3) Conversations with Arthur

He used to try to convince me that the existence of, the discovery of and the understanding of the relevance and possible uses of the irrational number which is commonly and internationally and historically known as Pi, that is, to five decimal places, the number 3.14159, is irrevocable proof of the existence of God. It's just so illogical, he told us, that it could ever work, that it must just prove that there's something more than us. And it's so incredible that we can discover it. That proves something. I think he's wrong. I told him. I think you're wrong. I told him, for somebody so palpably intelligent, Arthur, sometimes you think like your head's full of wool.    — Name of grandad.

He liked me. He never got too cross. We'd talk about beer together. He never bothered about me coming from – He watched an unusual amount of tennis. Everything was tennis with him. His conversation was peppered with tennis metaphors. Sometimes I'd watch tennis with him. I never liked it much.

Is it a terrible thing to say that sometimes the company of men is kind of, in some way, comforting? I don't mean it to sound. You know? I don't mean anything other than –

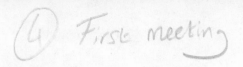

(4) First meeting

He had a house in the eastern suburbs of Toulon in a town called Carquerraine. In the south of fucking France for fuck's sake.

When I go there with Helen for the first time we drive in her car. She's a kind of mix between being a bit embarrassed because, ostensibly at least, at the time we're kind of, what? Socialists? And just being really fucking proud because her dad has a house in the South of France and she's taking me there and she's paying for the ferry because I'm skint. She keeps going on about how odd he is but how she has a feeling that she thinks I'll like him.

And I do.    Helen is wife?

She says that's one of the things she likes about me. I like people. People like me. They think I'm gentle. I had absolutely no idea that people thought I was gentle. And she says she really likes this bit.

*He shows the area at the top of his arm.*    (5)    The best part of a man

This bit is one of the best bits of a man, she says. Which is a phrase that just about sends me completely insane with love for her and her nose and her smile and everything.

Lucy was a Caesarean. And when Helen was in labour there was a moment when I thought she could have died. And I am a little bit embarrassed now because I had to go into the toilets to change into my, what are they called? Scrubs is it? When I had to change into my scrubs I did have a bit of a cry. And when I did, I did ask God, who I don't fucking think is even there in the first place, to make sure that Helen was all right. I said we can survive if we lose the baby but I don't think I could make it if she went and died on me. It's like talking to a photograph or the mirror. It has the same effect. Which isn't to discount it completely, but it's not God.    (6)

The second time I go to his house, after we've been going out now for two years, he takes me diving. He's become a big fan of scuba-diving in the eighteen months that me and Helen have been going out, which is maybe a surprising character    (7)

(6) Lucy      (7) Second visit    Lucy is my daughter

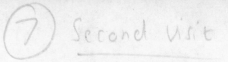

development in a man of his age but he's a surprising man. Between St Tropez and the Île de Porquerolles there are, he says, actual shipwrecks that you can actually dive on. Would I like to come?

I've never worn a wetsuit before and it takes me longer to get into than I'd hoped and it makes me feel a bit fat.

He tells me he's going to take me to the Sea Wall. I ask him, 'The what?' He says, 'The Sea Wall.' This makes no sense to me at all. There's a wall in the sea? It drops down. Hundreds of feet. I had no idea that the bed of the sea was built like that. I thought it was a gradual slope. He'd brought us these little bags with bits of bread in and you hold them upside down to swim with so you don't lose the bread because it naturally floats upwards. And he takes us to the wall. And swimming there, with the sun, even bright as it is above us, and it is a bright day. Even then the darkness of the fall that the wall in the sea reveals is as terrifying as anything I've seen.

You get back to the surface of course and the idea that there ever wasn't a sea wall down there in the first place is a bit embarrassing, frankly. I mean, what did I actually think the seabed was made of?

When Helen's giving birth to Lucy the midwife calls to me, 'Daddy, do you want to see your baby born?' They've built a little tent. I look over the edge of the tent and I, you know I'm one of those people who, I never know where to look when people point things out to me. Like I'm a kid and I'm driving along and Mum says, 'Look! A kestrel!' Or, 'Look! A plane!' and I don't have the faintest idea what to look at. I just smile and nod dumbly and say, 'Oh yeah!' but I'm completely lying. And this is a bit like that. Mainly I see the yellow of the inside of her stomach. Once you've seen the inside of somebody's stomach, I think your relationship with that person probably then moves to what? A new level?

I love her completely. With every bone and bit of skin of me. And it's been very rare the times in our relationship when

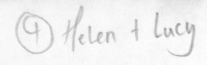

she's cried and I've comforted her. I'm fucking crying all the fucking time. I can't watch an episode of *ER* without just being a wreck. I cry at *Ground Force* when the person comes back and they've had their garden done up as a surprise.

We go there, to his house, for our holidays every year. We did used to drive. Three years straight we drove all the way down from London without stopping. We took it in turns driving. We kind of promised to share navigating but neither of us needed any help. We did it fine.

When Lucy was born we started flying there though, because the driving's not fair on a baby and he'd buy us the tickets. You can get flights to Carcassonne for dead cheap but he'd pay for us to fly into Nice and he'd hire us a car when we got there.

The first time he sees her he takes her by surprise a bit. He looms over from behind her and he's wearing his glasses, these big old glasses, and he's a very, very tall man, and he takes her by surprise and she screams like living shit, believe me.

It took her about three weeks to recover from that. But she did.

And then she'd start with the shuffling across the floor to reach him and putting her hands up and making these little noises that basically mean, 'put me on your lap and read me a story now, you funny old fucker, I don't care if you're meant to be weird, I don't care if you're meant to be scary, I don't care what anybody fucking thinks about you, I want a story and I want it now.' Who could resist that?

She starts wearing cardigans and that's me done for.

One time I say to him, 'If there's a God? Is he a man?' and the question catches him by surprise a bit. But after a while he says that, yes, he thinks in the end God is probably a man. So I say to him, 'What does he look like? Does He have a beard? Does He wear robes? Does He have long white hair?' He says to me that the thing about God is that

whatever I think He looks like, well, He will look the absolute opposite to that. And whatever I think He is least likely to look like, then that is what He will look like. So I ask him if he means God looks a bit like Gary Glitter and he tells me not to be so bloody silly. So I say to him, 'If you can't tell me what He looks like, if you don't know what He looks like and He doesn't look like anything, then how do you know He is anything more than just an idea? Just something you made up?'

She's eight. We've been going every year. We've talked for years about having a second child but every time we talk about it we think about Lucy and we just think, you know what? We're very happy. She's just. We just want her.

She's clever. She's funny. She's very, very pretty. She's Helen's sidekick. She's my sweetheart. They make little wisecracks about me. The two of them stand there sizing me up but I know if they push it too far that she'll come running over to me and put her arms around me because the idea of properly making me sad makes her feel a little bit sick.

In the eight years that she's been born I've fucked a lot of things up and somehow by the skin of my teeth managed to largely come out unscathed. And me and Helen. We're doing OK. We have little routines and stuff, like about the dishwasher or the shopping or cooking, because I really like to cook for her but compared to her I'm shit at it. So when she cooks it's properly a treat. We have all these routines but it's like we fucking love them. Rather than finding them, what? Restricting?

Sometimes when you swim in the sea the force of the waves can crash right against you. It can knock you over. There have been times when just trying to get out of the sea I've been knocked over. Two summers ago this happened and I cracked my coccyx against a stone on the shore's edge and flailed about like some kind of huge seal. I was at that moment the mathematical polar opposite of Daniel Craig.

It doesn't get like this normally where he is. Normally the sea's warm there. Which is quite an unusual feeling for me.

I always swim out as far as I think is safe and then turn and swim another ten strokes and then stop and swim back.

Sometimes you think the tide's caught you. You panic because you think you're not moving. You are. You just need to turn on your back. Collect your breathing. Kick slowly. You're moving.

I ask him, 'Where is He?' He says,' Who?' I say, 'God. Where is He? Is He in the sky? That's where people used to think He was. Children and medieval people. Is He on the edge of our solar system? Is He on the edge of our galaxy? Because every time we think we've located where He must be then we find out something else and we realise that God can't be there. Is He fifteen billion light years away? On the very edges of the universe? In the parts of the universe that take on the form of the time of the Big Bang? That have that kind of density? Is He there? Is that where He is?'

He says, 'We don't know everything, Alex. There are some things we don't know. There are things we can't explain.' I tell him, 'Now.' He says, 'What?' I say, 'We can't explain them now but that doesn't mean that they have no reason. It just illustrates the gaps in our knowledge. It doesn't mean we won't be able to explain them one day because I really, because I think we will.'

I want to acknowledge something. And it's embarrassing because I know it's something that you will have noticed. There's a hole running through the centre of my stomach. You must have all felt a bit awkward because you can probably see it. Even in this light. Mostly people choose not to talk about it. Some people tell me that they're sorry but that, yes, they can see my hole. 'What's that, Alex?' they say. 'You appear to have a great big hole running right through the middle of you.'

_13 The Second Coming_

_14 The Hole_

I'd started doing OK. You know? I'd got a, it sounds stupid, but I got a contract with British Home Stores. I took the photographs for their catalogues. And for their websites. The menswear. The womenswear. The back-to-school stuff. The homewear. I made so much money from taking photographs of cushions and saucepans and digital alarm clocks I can barely believe it myself.

Five weeks ago, just before we go. Just before all the packing and the frantic stuff about what are we going to take, Helen's buying some stuff to take with us. She's got Lucy all her new stuff. Her dresses and her cossie and her books and toys for the flight. And she got me some shades which were properly pucker, seriously. Very Poncherello. From Chips. And she asks me to come into the bedroom because there's something she wants to show me. And I get there and she's wearing this dress. It's a blue dress. With this dropped back. She asks me to tell her what I think. I swear for about thirty seconds I couldn't speak. She looked. Oh. And the idea that I was married to her. And that we had our girl. And this was our life.

There's a man in the market in Port Grimaud that we visit on our second day and he sells us a case of claret for the equivalent of about fifteen quid and it is like heaven. We drink two bottles on our second night there.

The next day Helen has to go to the supermarket because we need to get some bread and some shampoo for Lucy and I need some athlete's foot cream, and we love, they have these little yogurts, these little pots of vanilla-flavoured yogurt that you can't get in Britain. And she wants to get some cheese. It's fun getting it from the market, but as it goes it's a proper rip-off so she wants to go to the supermarket, which is where most of the French people go anyway.

So me and Arthur go down with Lucy, down to the sea. There's a bay just near his house. And round the corner from the bay there's a little cove that you can climb on to. And when the bay's busy you can go to this cove, which is actually nearer his house and more secluded, and it's very quiet and it's lovely and we talk about it and we decide to go there.

She can go into this world. Did you ever know any kids like that? When she thinks nobody's looking she can start off just going further and further into her imagination. Playing games all by herself. Actually, what she's really doing is she's talking to herself, which some people might find a bit disconcerting, but I just love to watch her.

He says to me one time, he looks at me and he says, 'He's in the feeling of water. Sometimes there's the shape of the roll of land. He's in the way some people move. He's in the light falling over a city at the start of an evening. He's in the space between two numbers.'

You know what the cruellest thing I ever did to anybody was? I'll tell you.

I've started getting into detective fiction. I have a friend who works at St Mary's University and he said to me, 'Alex, all fiction is detective fiction.' He's completely wrong. Jane Austen isn't detective fiction. Franz Kafka isn't detective fiction. *Bridget Jones* isn't detective fiction. Detective fiction is detective fiction. James Ellroy. Arthur goes for a swim. I'm reading *LA Noir*. The bit where the cop and the killer are in the deserted car park meeting at midnight with the lights out, neither knowing whether the other is there. Lucy's kind of being a Power Ranger.

The sun is gorgeous. I've got my shades on it's so bright.

He comes back. 'The water's amazing,' he says. He dries off. I notice his feet. The skin on his feet is unusually battered and cracked. It's one of the moments you kind of rumble that he's a little old. He tells me I can go for a swim.

I do. And the water *is* amazing. I wade past the first bank. I get past all the seaweed and I swim out and out and out. Around the bay. And the light. At that time of day light on the Mediterranean is – and the sea is warm. I turn round.

I'm about twenty yards out. The sky is this huge blue curve.
I can see the houses on the top of the road. I can see his
house. I can see the swimmers round the corner of the bay.
I can see Arthur sitting reading. He's reading some history
of China. He's really into it. His towel draped around his
legs. Water dripping onto his book. I can see all that from
here, with real detail. I can see Lucy playing behind him.
Running about a bit. Playing Power Rangers.

I can watch them as she does a little bit of a jump. It's odd
because he's so into his book that he doesn't notice that she
loses her footing on the sand and the gravel of the rock and
she slips and stumbles. And she's quite close to a little edge
of one of the rocks there and what she does is she tries to
correct her balance but in trying to correct the balance of
her weight she actually puts more weight on her back foot
that slips out from underneath her and it's weird to look at
because she does fall off the edge of this six-foot-high cliff
on the rocks and she falls backwards and cracks her head
against some rocks which are jutting out at the bottom of
the cliff.

I can see it all clearly but I can't really hear anything and it's
weird watching it with no sound. Like if the sound's off on
the telly it's always a bit strange. It takes a while to register
before I turn and swim back to the shore.

I'm not thinking so I start swimming faster and faster, which
is stupid because I'm panicking and when you panic you
can't really breathe properly so I have to tell myself,
concentrate on your breathing.

I can kind of watch him between strokes and he's thrown
down his book and jumped off the cliff and there's one other
couple there that I didn't notice before who have stopped
their sunbathing and run towards where she is. And I notice
him pick her up.

He's torn between running back to the house to call an
ambulance and waiting for me.

I get there in enough time for him not to have to worry about this for too long.

I go to her. I take her from him. There is, what there is, which is surprising to me, is there is a handful of blood in her hair. It's thick and matted and her hair is all chewed up by it.

I read that it's a process. That it's never absolutely instantaneous. The injury causes the death of brain cells so signals are no longer sent to the lungs and bit by bit the machine closes down.

Her blood sticks to my hands.

I carry her up the path of the cove and I haven't bothered getting dried and people are looking at me. Stopping still in their tracks and talking to me in French and I'm aware that I'm kind of not crying, I look like, fuck, I don't know. I go back into the house with her and as I'm getting through the sliding glass doors I bang her head against the wall and I'm talking to her, which is stupid, and I tell her I'm sorry for hitting her head but there is part of me that's thinking, well, fuck it now. What does it fucking matter now? I may as well drag her by her fucking ankle. This bit of meat. This bit of meat and air.

I remember I was a bit astonished because one of the ambulance men spoke English. Quite good English. He'd lived in Southampton and I couldn't help thinking, 'Why the fuck did you live in Southampton of all places?'

The sound of her closing the door with her bags full of yogurt and shampoo and cheese and bread takes me completely by surprise. She looks at me across his house. She's wearing sunglasses to protect her against the light.

Oh Jesus fuck.

He's sitting on his sofa. He's still wrapped in his towel. He is a man that is completely broken. He is a shattered form. The little noises he makes.

I leant over the desk at the check-in at Nice and we'd been taken to the front of the queue and we had actually been given an upgrade and while the woman there was sorting all this out I looked over her at the sheet she was checking off on her desk and there was a list of the passengers and the crew and the baggage and at the end of the list it read 'human remains'. Which was a bit –

We're sitting, the three of us, in the departure lounge. We can't really touch one another. We can't look at each other or at anybody else. I turn to him, and this is the cruellest thing I ever did to anybody else, and don't forget this is a man I, you know, I've known him for ten years and I, I, I do, I love him. I look at him. I say to him –

You get back to London and the noise of the place and the dirt and the colour and the roar of it. I can't actually. What I can't really do, for now, at least, is work. There's a lie at the heart of photography that I've always cherished. When you take a photograph what you do is you freeze something that's actually alive. To do this properly you need, more than anything, to believe in life.

There's a child outside the window laughing. And in his laugh there is absolutely no joy or humour.

Warning: this vehicle is reversing.

I have a complete and total inability to cry.

You see people when they say to you that they can't imagine not believing in anything because it would be just too depressing. I think there's something sick about that. The level of cowardice in that is just unbearable to me.

I've been home for three weeks.

If this can happen, anything can happen.

*He goes to a window. He opens it. Looks out for a short time. Looks back.*

Just now there was this couple outside and they were arguing in the street and it looked like they were deliberately trying to copy characters out of soap operas. In the way that they argued. As though the closest they'll ever get to being famous is rowing in the street like they were actually on *EastEnders*. The misery and the emptiness and the vacuous fucking shitness of their lives is so considerable that the proximity to the behaviour of soap characters acts as some kind of consolation.

Helen moves around the house.

I'm holding my entire head together. The skin and the shell of me. I'm falling absolutely inside myself. But you can see that. You can see the – in my –

Just because we don't know doesn't mean we won't know. We just don't know yet. But I think one day we will. I think we will.

*He exits.*